Space Chase
Book 1:
Arrendrallendriania

(A-ren-DRA-len-dree-AH-nee-ya)

AKA: "They call me Arren."

By Dr Joseph Ireland
"Dr Joe"

Space Chase - Arrendrallendriania

Space Chase - Arrendrallendriania

Big thanks to my wife and daughters, my family, and to all my readers!

And to science for her majestic contributions and challenging ideas for society!

Buy your own copy at www.DrJoe.id.au!

Front cover and inside art by Nathan Clark
newnclark29@hotmail.com

Back cover art by Simun Pavic
zhika811.deviantart.com

Edited by www.adroitediting.com.au

Published 21 August 2015 by Creating Science by Dr Joe.
© Dr Joseph Ireland, 2012
© Dr Joseph Ireland, 2015
© Girl's Space cover edition, 2018, 2019
All rights reserved. Reasonable portions of this work may be used for educative purposes.

All characters appearing in this work are fictitious. Any resemblance to real persons, living or dead, is purely coincidental.

Do not attempt any activities or experiments in this book without competent adult supervision. Science is dangerous.

ISBN: 978-0-6484941-2-6
Also ISBN-13: 978-1516993543 (CreateSpace-Assigned)
BISAC: Fiction / Science Fiction / General

Feedback and comments welcome – www.drjoe.id.au

Contents

Chapter 1 The worth of a broken rocket launcher 1

Chapter 2 The girl from outer space 11

Chapter 3 And *that* is why we keep secrets
from the Earthlings! 25

Chapter 4 Leaving Earth 41

Chapter 5 The garden 66

Chapter 6 Cambriania 80

Chapter 7 Rlaeiul 92

Chapter 8 How *not* to make friends
in the Universal Unity 102

Chapter 9 Tauroo 110

Chapter 10 Inside a Nova Class high-end multidimensional
Universal Unity Star craft 122

Chapter 11 When now you know what it was you never
knew you never knew 131

Chapter 12 The day the Coebri Pirates came to Ms
Garibaldi's garden 139

End of Book 1 *and* Start of Book 2
Freedom and Rockets 155

What Ms Garibaldi said 163

About the author 165

Space Chase - Arrendrallendriania

All footnotes are available as live links at

www.drjoe.id.au

Make sure you check with your parent or guardian first

Chapter 1
The worth of a broken rocket launcher

This time, he was sure he'd win.

"Hey *Looser!*" Mark T mocked him. "Just you wait till you see what I've got *this* time. You're gonna lose, *again!*"

Chase scowled at the big bully. They were on the school oval, on a Sunday, when they shouldn't have been. Mark T had his two buddies from class with him and Chase only had his twin brother, Lucky. That really was their names, their dad being a mad hippy and all.

As per the rules, all non-competitors sat on top of the school sport shed judging the contest. If Mr Twain, the sports teacher, had seen them on the tall shed roof where they shouldn't have been, he'd have had an apocalyptic fit.

"No cheating this time," Lucky called from the shed. He had wavy blond hair, a smidgeon of freckles, and was built healthy: he never seemed to run out of energy. It was what always got him into trouble with the teachers, his constant fidgeting, and now they were in high school he'd stopped trying to sit still and got in trouble almost every day. Always fidgeting and never studying; Chase's exact opposite in almost every way. Though to be fair, Chase knew his twin also had a kind heart, and it kept Chase and some of the other small kids safe from bullies.

Bullies like Mark Treadworth; who insisted on being called Mark T so he wasn't confused with any of the other Marks in the world. Chase would have never had the courage to face Mark T without his brother.

"I don't *need* to cheat," Mark T teased him. He was almost a head taller than every other student in class; a big, muscly kid who was heavier than a cow and had big bricks for hands. Even the teachers steered clear of him. But what was worse, he wasn't one of those dumb bullies who never got anywhere in life. He was smart, but never did any work yet still got full marks! He was right into Pokémon and hacking into other people's Facebook accounts. In short, he was a great big jerk.

Chase tried not to obsess about how Mark T usually won at everything, and instead focused on making a last minute check over his latest addition to the rocket contest[1]. It had started friendly enough, some little demonstration the teacher did in class launching a rocket using little tablets dissolved in water. Then Chase had suggested using vinegar but Mark T had told everyone that was dumb and they should use petrol.

Well, no one was a stupid enough to use petrol, but the competition was on! Chase was the only other acknowledged science genius in their class, but unlike Mark T he'd never gotten a big head over it. Still, every year since grade two he'd had to play second fiddle to Mark T and now that he was aged thirteen and ¾ he was over it.

So the competition was on. Winner took five dollars.

Mark had brought a soft drink bottle, vinegar and bi-carb. It was pretty obvious what he was up to. He was going to get the chemicals to react to create carbon dioxide gas that would power his rocket.

Chase, however, had decided on a more mechanical solution. He and his brother had taken a ball pump and

---

[1] Check out www.DrJoe.id.au for video and instructions on building this as well as heaps of other science activities!

pushed the end through a big wine cork they'd found lying around the house. The idea was to set up a soft drink bottle in a stand, attach the ball pump, and pump like crazy. Prelaunch testing had shown Chase that decorations on the bottle, such as launch doors and windows, just slowed it down. So he opted for a simple aerodynamic rocket cap to help it achieve maximum height and with a dozen launches up to the top of their roof, he was ready to go.

Mark T was just smiling; his beady, greedy eyes on them both.

"Who's first?" Lucky called. He was sitting next to one of the other boys from science class. They usually got along pretty well even though he was part of Mark T's gang, or one of Mark's *lackeys* as Lucky liked to call them.

"Loser goes first," Mark T said, indicating towards Chase.

"We'll see who the loser's going to be this time!" Chase called back, almost angry enough to throw the bottle right at his head.

Mark T just laughed. He seemed to like making people angry.

Chase set up his rocket, pressing the cork in with all his strength. He pumped as fast as he could, trying to beat the air hissing out from the tiny holes around the edge. The air pressure inside built up as more and more air poured into the bottle, and after a few seconds there was a satisfying *POP* and the rocket shot upwards, curled left, and made it almost to the height of the sports shed roof.

"Ha, beat that!" Lucky said, punching the air in triumph.

Mark T stared down his nose at Chase and smiled a wicked smile.

He poured a cup of vinegar into his bottle and then pushed a roll of tissue paper filled with bi-carb. He then shoved a rubber stopper in as hard as he could and held the bottle out in front of him.

"Beat this, space nerd," he said.

A second later the bubbling, fizzing mix exploded from the base of the bottle, sending the rocket up high in the air, at least a full story higher than Chase's bottle[2]. The twins stared at it in amazement.

"I win!" Mark gloated.

Chase bit his lip. He was so upset that he almost burst into tears. But he'd learnt long ago to never show anyone how he really felt. He didn't have many friends, but at least he never got hurt. With trembling hands he handed over the five dollars.

"There's a good boy..." Mark T mocked. He sniffed the money and then punched his fists together. "Now, *snotface*, I'm going to teach you a lesson for loosing. Boys, get 'em!"

For a moment everyone just stood looking at each other, not sure of what to do. Then Lucky must have decided Mark T was serious, and before anyone else could move he'd slid all the way down the roof and jumped onto the pile of long grass next to the sport shed that nobody ever seemed to mow.

"Hey, that's not fair!" protested Chase.

"I don't fight fair!" Mark T roared and reached out to grab him.

Well, everyone knew better than to let Mark T get a hold of them, and Chase was just a little bit smarter than most. So quick as lightning he dipped down and grabbed his rocket launcher. In a second, Lucky was there and they were running off as fast as they could across the oval.

---

[2] Why do you think Mark's rocket worked so much better than Chase's? Both used air pressure...

Mark T was slow, that was obvious, but his lackeys weren't. One of them almost grabbed a hold of Lucky but he jumped sideways and the boy missed and went sliding into the dust. His buddy stopped to help him up.

"This way," Lucky said.

They were running towards old Ms Garibaldi's garden.

Well, junkyard really, thought Chase. Ms Garibaldi was a crazy old Italian lady who owned half an acre of land pressed right up next to the school. She had some kind of hoarding disorder and so had filled her entire yard wall to wall with junk till it had become an unfathomable maze of trash and treasure, mostly trash. Every now and then some kid would get brave enough to try and save two minutes on their way to school by cutting through her yard. If the teachers found out, they got detention. If Ms Garibaldi found out, she'd force the poor kid to have tea and dry, powdery scones with her while she talked about her grandchildren, and everyone agreed that that punishment was *far worse!*

But, Chase reasoned, *when being chased by Mark T and his gang there are certain things worth the risk.*

Chase followed Lucky over the fence and they were hidden among her trash in seconds. They ran along two neat isles of teapots and old tires, hoping they would lose Mark T and get back home before their dad found out they'd been trespassing.

Not that he will mind, Chase thought ruefully. Their dad didn't appear to care if they came home each day, didn't even seem to know if they were in their beds at night. He'd never been the same since Mum left suddenly, when Chase and Lucky were only four years old. He could remember a time when dad used to smile, but that was a long time ago now.

Chase heard Mark's gang swearing as they crossed the fence.

"Idiots, Ms Garibaldi will hear them," Lucky said.

"I can't believe he tried to punch me," Chase replied.

"I can. He's just like that. I didn't think he'd win the rocket contest though. He's such an *idiot*," Lucky said.

"He's not an idiot," Chase muttered.

Sure enough, Mark T soon managed to snoop out the correct way that they'd tried to escape and they had to hurry off again. They snuck past some old buckets and a wall of bottle caps, only just a little bit ahead of the bullies. Soon they came to a bit of a clearing in the old junkyard with a rusty old metal table that might have looked quite ornate once. It was accompanied by a steel framed deck chair, its plastic covering old and sun bleached, but they were propped up to form a formal seating arrangement. And behind all that was an enormous thatched wooden chest.

A *huge* thatched chest, gigantic, the size of a short dumpster. It could easily fit both of them inside, and still leave enough room to scamper away if the bullies found them. It had a lid made out of palm leaves woven together, and sides made of woven wood sticks and ornate panels with plenty of holes for spying.

Lucky and Chase got the same idea at the same time.

"Quick, in here," Lucky whispered.

Mark's gang was getting closer.

But just as Chase was dashing past the old table he knocked his hand, sending his rocket platform flying. He went to grab it but Lucky pulled him back.

"No time!" Lucky whispered.

As quick as they could they jumped into the old wooden chest. It smelt like Indonesia, with rich wooden lacquer and strange, foreign spices. They took up positions spying through the sewn wooden sides.

A second later Mark T entered the clearing, his breathing heavy. His lackeys followed after, looking frantic and belligerent.

Suddenly Chase's heart sank as Mark T, and Mark alone, spotted his fallen rocket launcher.

"Look at this, guys!" Mark T called.

"They went this way!" One of the lackeys insisted, pointing the way the rocket launcher had fallen.

"I doubt it…" Mark T said, his voice cunning. He was looking around everywhere, looking around with his beady, greedy, envious eyes.

"Oh cr-" Lucky whispered.

"Ma che c'e'?" An old woman's voice suddenly called from nearby among the organised garbage.

"Ms Garibaldi. Run!" One lackey shouted and they scampered away.

Mark T edged away, but smiled his cruel grin.

"I know you're here Chase. You lose again, you'll *always* lose, maggot!" He said and twisted the launcher in his bare, beefy hands until it was completely broken.

A moment later Ms Garibaldi stormed into the clearing.

"Ui, ragazzo! Vai via, subito!" She called, shooing him away like a fly.

He laughed in her face and walked slowly away.

"Scemo," she muttered.

Lucky and Chase sighed a great sigh of relief.

She picked up the broken rocket launcher, turning it over in her hands and examining it.

The boys looked at each other, wondering what she was thinking.

Next thing they knew she put it on a shelf with dozens of other sculptures and pieces of junk. Perhaps, Chase wondered, she thought it was hers? Or perhaps she was keeping it as a trophy of the day she'd chased off the tyrant Mark T?

Then she sat down.

"Oh, you've got to be kidding," Lucky whispered.

It was good her hearing wasn't so great.

"Questi figli mi fanno sempre stancare," she muttered in her strange language. She patted her brow with a handkerchief, crossed her hands and began to doze off.

Lucky nudged Chase, indicating it was time to leave.

"I'm not going out there," he whispered.

"We'll have to, we can't stay in here," Lucky argued.

"We'll have to wait till she falls asleep," Chase said.

"But that could be–" Lucky began.

"Che cosa?" The old lady muttered, opening her eyes and looking around.

Neither of them moved. Chase didn't really care if she made them eat scones and tea, but he didn't want to get in trouble by Dad or the school for trespassing, *especially* on a Sunday. So they waited. It took almost twenty minutes of twitching and scratching for Ms Garibaldi to fall asleep.

The sun was getting quite low in the sky. Still, Dad was usually so out of it he probably wouldn't care, but Chase was getting hungry.

"Now?" He muttered. His legs numb from sitting.

Lucky took a careful look, creaking the lid open just a fraction.

Ms Garibaldi didn't stir.

He nodded.

As silent as a breeze they opened up the chest and helped each other out.

Lucky began walking back the way they came but Chase looked around. He wanted his launcher back. He'd fix it up, find out what went wrong, and then he'd beat Mark T for good. He'd make *him* cry with shame for trying to beat him up today.

"What're you doing?" Lucky whispered, the worry clutching at his voice.

Chase didn't answer, just indicated to him to keep quiet.

"Chase," Lucky nagged, hiding in fear by the far end of a shelf full of old books.

Ms Garibaldi snored but did not wake up.

As careful as was humanly possible Chase snuck up to the trophy shelves and grabbed hold of his broken launcher. It was twisted terribly and would take hours to fix. He started to pull it out but a broken metal wire scratched the shelf, making a loud screeching noise.

Ms Garibaldi did not stir.

Chase placed his hand over the offending wire, bent it down and, just as gently as if he was holding a butterfly, and prised it from the shelf. It made a gentle *ping* sound as he lifted it off but Ms Garibaldi still did not move. He breathed out a huge sigh of relief without even realising he was holding his breath.

Then the junkyard *exploded*.

A huge pillar of green flame tore down in the twilight sky. Shelves shook and fell over left and right. Papers scattered in all directions and the enormous BOOM it made caused their clothes to vibrate like at a school concert.

Lucky and Chase were thrown to the ground.

"Are you alright?" Chase asked his brother out loud.

"Yeah," Lucky replied, "What was that?"

Suddenly a terrible grating sound, like a pig dying of a cold, snorted out from behind them and they turned around in terror.

But it was Ms Garibaldi, covered in fallen trophies and face blacked with soot, completely, and safely, fast asleep.

Chapter 2
The girl from outer space

"Is she dead?" Lucky asked, almost brave enough to poke the sleeping Ms Garibaldi on the head.

"Dead people don't snore," Chase replied.

"What do you think caused that explosion?"

"I don't know, but I'm going to find out." He said, looking over at the smouldering crater.

"Are you *crazy!*" Lucky whispered, "It could be a nuclear bomb for all we know. I want to get out of here while she's still asleep." He jerked his hand back at Ms Garibaldi like he wanted to poke her out of the picture altogether.

"But I'm curious…" Chase tried to explain.

"You're *always* curious! Curious enough to set fire to the kitchen curtains, curious enough to grow wild peas in the back yard, curious enough to try and beat Mark T at a rocket contest. *Curse* you and your scientific curiosity!" He complained.

But Chase was not deterred. He had a question, and questions needed answers!

He crawled out from under a dangerously tilting bookshelf and there, lying at the bottom of a smouldering two meter deep crater, was a space ship. A real genuine UFO. It was pointy at one end, sharp like a knife, but got really fat at the other end, making it look a bit like a flat tipped egg, or maybe a tear drop if it was turned side on. It was smooth too, like it might be designed to cut through the atmosphere with ease. It was silver, but pitted and scratched so that it wasn't shiny at all. It wasn't very large though; only big enough to fit a grown-up in if they were lying down, with room to stretch out a little perhaps.

Chase found himself torn between an overwhelming curiosity to find out more, and an almost insane desire to run screaming.

"Do you think there are any creatures in there?" Lucky whispered.

"I wonder if they survived the crash?" Chase asked.

Suddenly the UFO decided to answer them. There was a gentle crack and then a hiss like air escaping from a newly opened Coke can. An oval opening appeared along the top and it swung out and upwards like a door.

And out of it stumbled a girl, about their age, coughing and waving away the smoke that tumbled out of the space ship with her. She staggered up the slope toward them, but didn't appear to see them. Then she stood up, turned around, and looking at her spaceship said one word: "Ordya!"

Chase looked over at his brother, wondering what she meant, but he seemed to have no idea either. He watched her as she examined her spaceship. Her hair was dark and curly, her skin was a gentle brown. She might have had grey, or green eyes, it was a bit difficult to tell while she was climbing up. She looked like she was wearing some kind of skin-tight alien suit with odd harnesses and pockets around her, tattered fabric wound around her arms for homemade gloves. She was about their height, and her hands were poised on her hips in a very girly manner as she surveyed her downed ship, tutting and mumbling to herself in some language he didn't recognise at all.

Lucky hit Chase on the arm and nodded in her direction, seeming to indicate that he should say hello.

Chase shook his head, Lucky was the one always getting into trouble or saying hello to new people, so he hit him on the arm to indicate that *he* should be the one to say hello.

Lucky slapped him on the back of the head and indicated something along the lines of 'except in the case of visitors from outer space.'

This did not impress Chase, who poked his brother in the chest and mouthed, 'no'.

Then in an act of complete stupidity, Lucky pulled Chase's hair.

It was on. They slapped and wacked each other for a good three seconds. That is, until the girl turned around.

Chase and Lucky paused mid-slap.

Then she screamed, Lucky yelled, and Chase bellowed.

Then old Ms Garibaldi snorted.

They froze, the three of them just looking at each other.

That was when Chase got his first good look at her. Her face looked perfect, like it was carved from some kind of pure alien stone. Her eyes were the most beautiful mysterious green eyes he'd ever seen, the iris's filled with strange patterns he desperately wanted to study closer. Her lips…

"Hello," Lucky interrupted his thoughts.

"He low?" She repeated, her brow creased in concentration.

She didn't look frightened at all now, though they'd no doubt startled her with the violent announcement of their presence. Chase decided it was safe to speak to her.

"Hello? Do you speak English?" He asked.

"Dyoo speek?" She repeated.

"English, English!" Lucky said loudly.

It didn't look like Ms Garibaldi was going to wake up any time soon. It seemed to Chase that she could sleep through an earthquake while lying on a bed of those cheap electronic toys from McDonalds.

"English," she finally said in a perfect accent like a Google dictionary. "Yes."

"Oh. Well then," Lucky replied, getting confident and leaning on his arm the way he did when he was trying to flirt with girls. "I'm Lucky, that's my name. And this is my little brother Chase."

Chase felt indignant, Dad had never told them who was born first. He'd also given them alternate first names that he'd never told them about, something do with some form of Wiccan name protection thingy.

"Hey, you don't know who was born first!" Chase argued.

"Sure, like *you're* the oldest," Lucky mocked him, head dangling to the side in sarcasm.

Chase felt like hitting his brother yet again but, given the present company, decided against it. Ignoring his immature brother, he turned to the girl and said, "I'm Chase."

"Chase." The girl smiled, and Chase found his heart suddenly seemed to be having trouble keeping a regular beat.

"She might speak English, but she doesn't seem to speak it very well," Lucky muttered.

"What's your name?" Chase said, trying not to blush.

She spat the whole thing out like it was a huge sentence crammed into a single word, "Arrendrallendriania."

"Arrend, areendari," Chase attempted.

"We'll call you Arren," Lucky decided.

"But that's not her name!" Chase argued. He didn't like being inaccurate, but Lucky never seemed to care.

"Like it matters. Hey Arren, what'ya doing here? Not part of an invasion force are you?"

"Invasion... NO!" She said, looking around. Then she looked like she thought she was being a bit silly. "No, no invasion me. Not. I am no an invasion. I hidding, *hiding*.

Must needs to hide," she said, and put her finger across her mouth like she was trying to make them whisper, then looked at them hopefully as if she wasn't sure she'd gotten the gesture right.

"Yeah, us too," Lucky agreed.

"How are you going to hide something like that?" Chase asked her, pointing at her spaceship.

"Mmm? Oiya!" She said in her strange language. She scurried down the slope and began talking to her spaceship, waving her hand as if to shut the door. It seemed reluctant to help out, but with several jerky motions it finally closed. Then she gave it an affectionate pat and it began to fade away.

"How are you doing that?" Chase wondered in amazement.

She tried to tell him in her own language, waving her hands around as if something was trying to bend around something else.

"You mean the light bends around the ship, making it look invisible?"

She shook her head.

"No light, not light! Minrithal. Minrithal wo nabbatgot." She explained, flustered, making no sense to anyone at all except herself.

Then she crawled out of the crater and looked over at them.

"Dinner time!" She announced.

"Oh! You hungry? I hope she's not planning on eating us," Lucky joked.

"Yeah right, I wonder if she can even eat our food?" Chase asked.

"Well, we can always *experiment!*"

"I don't think it's ethical to go experimenting on the dietary limits of alien life forms without permission," Chase protested.

"Sure, go right ahead. The scientists will tell us all about the needs of her... metabolism right after they've finished *cutting her up!*"

"Ha, ha," Chase said sarcastically, then turned to the girl from outer space. "Well, I suppose if you're hungry you can come with us. We can fix you some dinner soon, if you're feeling brave enough."

She smiled but neither of them knew if she understood a word they were saying. So Chase motioned for her to follow. She waved her invisible spaceship goodbye and walked out after them.

"You don't suppose Ms Garibaldi will notice a big hole in her back garden?" Chase asked as they walked away towards their home.

"You kidding, this place is such a mess she probably loses her own way to the front door every other day!"

The three of them walked to Chase's home.

***

Chase was a little disappointed; Dad was really out of it again, talking to the invisible pixies in the front garden. They lived in a two bedroom house in the suburbs and it was covered with rainbow pennants, dream catchers and other things from their dad's crazy attempts at talking to spirits and other weird things. Their house was a mess but not like Ms Garibaldi's kind of mess. Their house was full of crystals, used incense sticks, and beads which hung from threads in each and every doorway to improve the Feng Shui.

It had been that way ever since they were four.

Dad had long, wispy hair that hung down to his waist and over his face as he stumbled around, muttering to himself. He wore an ancient tie dyed tee-shirt underneath an old dressing gown that should have been thrown out years ago. His tan pants were held on by a rickety old leather belt latched together with a huge buckle in the shape of a dragon that he'd forged himself before they were born. He didn't speak much and when he did he mumbled. He looked after them even less, which meant they had to look after themselves, but that gave Chase time for more experiments and Lucky more time to level up in Call of Duty again.

"Hey, Dad, we brought a friend home," Lucky announced as soon as they'd walked in.

"She might be staying the night," Chase added, trying to make it sound all casual.

They hadn't spoken to her at all on their way home and she seemed to be happy to walk behind them admiring all the sights, such as birds and telegraph poles.

To their surprise, Dad walked right up to them and took a good look at Arren.

"Hello, good sir," she said in perfect English. It was a bit surprising.

"Staying the night you say?" Dad said, sounding suspicious for the first time in years. Actually, sounding more than anything in years.

"If it pleases you," she replied and did a curtsey.

Lucky raised an eyebrow. Chase wondered as well, her English had certainly improved. She was a very quick learner it seemed.

"What's up with ..." He began, but then seemed to change his mind. "So, you're staying here tonight?"

They all nodded.

Dad sighed. "Very well then. But she'll have to sleep in my room. I'll take the couch."

Chase wasn't really surprised. Dad hadn't sleep in his own bed since, well, for a very long time.

"Thank you, very good sir," she said, still sounding a little strange.

Dad smiled.

"Well, I'd better go fix dinner then," he said and hurried out.

Chase was speechless, it was Sunday. Dad only ever made dinner on Mondays, and even then it was peanut butter and jam sandwiches, or sausages if he was feeling motivated. Dad *never* made dinner on Sunday.

"Wow. He's being nice. What did you do to him Arren?" Lucky asked her.

"Nice man," she said. "Father him yours?"

"Yes, he is our father," Chase translated, while answering her question.

"Sometimes..." Lucky muttered, resentment hidden under his humour.

"Well, would you like me to show you around then?" Chase offered, to change the mood.

"Ooh, show her this!" Lucky said, and leaping over the couch flipped on his console. It was his best friend, Chase observed, and he was always playing it. Lucky swiped some newspapers off the couch next to him so that Arren could sit down.

Arren however, looked unimpressed and stared down at the tiny screen with flashing lights.

"Right, your family got a plasma screen have they?" Lucky smiled.

"Or some kind of alien holographic projector ..." Chase began, but then Dad walked in.

"You're not allergic to anything are you dear?" He asked her.

She looked at Chase, then shook her head no.

"Oh, very good then." He shuffled out.

"Exit, Dad, stage right," Lucky joked without even looking away from his game. Then he shifted position on the couch and accidentally knocked the remote control to the ground. With a click the TV switched off and the remote popped open, spilling the batteries everywhere.

"No! Noooo," Lucky wailed, throwing himself to the floor in a desperate attempt to recapture the fleeing batteries as quickly as possible. "Quick, the game's still running!"

Chase sighed, and picking up the back of the case handed it to him. "Don't worry," he said.

"Don't...? *Please!*" Lucky disagreed. He was ramming in the batteries as quickly as he could, messing them up in random arrangements.

"You boys OK?" Dad asked from the kitchen.

"Sure," they chorused, hoping he wouldn't realise they'd broken the remote before they could fix it.

Chase snatched the controller off Lucky and set them in right. "See, easy when you don't panic," he said.

"You can talk," Lucky mumbled and took the remote back, but when he went to switch the TV on it still didn't work. He yelled in dismay and tried to rip the batteries out again.

"Now you're putting them in the wrong way!" Chase said getting frustrated and snatched the remote back.

Lucky grabbed the other half and looked like they were about to get into another fight when Arren walked up, calmly took the remote from them both and opened it. Then, using a tiny piece of aluminium foil from a take away container that'd been sitting on the floor for months, she wedged a tiny piece along the battery contacts. She put the batteries back in the same way Chase had put them and promptly switched the TV back on.

"Oh," said Lucky, then jumped back on his chair and grabbed the remote. "Hey, I only need a few more experience points …" He mumbled something else then said, "Thanks Arren!" Then went back to ignoring them.

Chase sighed and decided to take Arren on a tour around the house. He showed her where she was going to sleep and she seemed pretty happy about that. Then he showed her the bathroom and toilet, and she was absolutely fascinated by the way the water came out of the taps. He tried to tell her what the toilet was, but she didn't seem to recognise it. She didn't seem to like the smell though and who could blame her, no one ever cleaned it properly.

They passed by his and Lucky's room and he wasn't going to let her in because he didn't think his dad would approve, but she walked right in anyway.

"Oooh," she said.

The place was a mess: Two preteens with no mother. Lolly wrappers were still on the floor from last Easter, three months ago, and a two week old KFC box from when Dad couldn't be bothered cooking on a Monday. Even the little black ants had given up on it by now but Chase had found it fascinating to watch while they devoured leftover chicken in only two days.

But not the place you want to take a girl.

Arren stood there, transfixed by what she was seeing. She seemed utterly entranced and Chase began to wonder what she was looking at.

She looked down at his bed on the lower bunk. He and Lucky were supposed to swap each year but somehow that had gone out the window several years ago. There, lying on his pillow, was a little crocheted bunny his mother had made for him when he was only two. It was originally green. He didn't let anyone know he still kept it.

She reached out her hand and it suddenly leapt right up off the pillow. She took in her hand and had a good look at it.

"Yours," she said in a reverent way.

"Yes," he replied, pretty surprised at what he'd just seen. But then she walked towards him, watching the bunny, and holding it out pressed it right to his chest.

"Special," she said, and walked out of the room.

Chase was confused. How could she know all that? Besides, he didn't like being reminded of his mother so much. Even so, he placed the bunny very gently next to his pillow.

Suddenly his nose caught the scent of something new cooking, it smelt like chops... and steamed vegetables.

Vegies?

It *could not* be vegies!

By the time he caught up to the strange alien girl she was watching Lucky in the living room. Chase was about to say something when Dad called from the kitchen.

"Tea time!"

Lucky hit pause and leapt up, always thinking of his stomach first.

"Cool. Hey guys!" He called, like he wasn't worried about a thing, at least not about having dinner with an alien. It was like she was some kind of visitor from around the street, not the other side of the universe.

By the time they reached the kitchen, Dad had set the table like never before. Somehow he'd found enough food to make a full meal, including chops, vegies and reconstituted mashed potatoes. There was cordial to drink, Chase didn't know they had cordial, and Dad had even managed to dig up the old salt shaker.

It was like being a family again.

Lucky sat down and started eating noisily.

"Now, now, son, not until we say thanks," Dad said.

"Thanks Dad," Lucky mumbled with a mouth half-full of rehydrated potatoes.

"I always give thanks," Dad said, and sitting down, bowed his head. Chase followed his example and so did Lucky, smiling like it was a big joke. Arren took her cue and bowed her head as well.

Dad took a deep breath and spoke slowly, "Universe, we thank you for this abundance and ask you to bless this food for our bodies. And please bless our new friend tonight and help her get out of any trouble she may be in. Thank you."

Chase opened his eyes and looked at his still reverent father. What make him think she was in trouble?

Arren was staring at Dad intently.

"Prayer?" She asked.

"Of a sort," he replied.

"Of a sort…" She muttered, as though trying to work out what he meant. Then she looked down and smiled, taking a big bite of steamed vegetables. "Yummy!"

They ate in silence, for the most part. Dad did try and ask about Arren, but she didn't answer. Lucky made up a story about her being an exchange student from France but that she didn't speak French very well either. She was staying at a hostel in town but they were fixing it up so she needed to stay somewhere else for a few days. Dad didn't really seem to buy any of it but for whatever reasons he decided to let her stay.

After dinner they all watched TV and for the first time Chase could remember, they watched it together. Arren seemed fascinated, happy to watch whatever everyone else wanted to watch. It didn't seem long before it got late and Dad said they all should go to their beds.

Arren got up, smiled and walked into the bedroom.

Lucky moaned how grateful he was to be going anyway because there was nothing but junk on TV and was out in a second.

"Chase, got a moment?" Dad said, organising the papers on the floor.

Chase didn't really want to talk to Dad without Lucky around; Lucky was much better at lying. He sat back down on the arm chair.

"Take care of that girl at school tomorrow Chase," he said.

"What makes you say that, Dad?" He asked, trying to sound relaxed.

Dad was quiet for a long time.

"Just... let's just say..." He rolled his eyes, like there was something embarrassing he wanted to say but didn't know how. "Her presence is ... different, son. Almost... I dunno, 'alien'. Try not to get too caught up her business, if you know what I mean."

Chase didn't. It was a very cryptic comment, but it freaked him out. Perhaps Dad already knew that she'd arrived from 'France' in a space ship?

"Dad," Chase moaned. "Look, I'm not going to get caught up in her *business*," he said, moving is fingers in a bunny ears, quote-unquote kind of way.

Dad looked at him, looked right at him like for the first time in almost eight years. He ran his old hand through Chase's hair.

"We'll see," he said, and went back to TV.

Chapter 3
And *that* is why we keep secrets from the Earthlings!

"Chase," a girl's voice whispered.

He woke up so quick that he hit his head on the underside of his brother's bed.

"Oh! Sorry," she said.

It was Arren.

"Arren, what are you doing? It must be like six AM!"

"Five fifty eight AM, to be exact. I've been waiting all night. I need your help."

That was when he realised she was speaking near perfect English, with a local accent.

"Arren, when did you learn to speak proppa?" He asked.

"Last night, it's what I've been doing. Did you hit your head badly? Do you need the hospital?" She asked.

"Ok, you can speak," he said, rubbing his head. "But you might be missing some of the finer points of our culture, we don't go to hospital for a bump on the head."

She seemed genuinely relieved to hear that. "Oh, good. I need your help."

"Yeah, figured that."

"Whasit?" Lucky muttered in his sleep.

They looked at him, then Chase got out of bed and wrapped a blanket around himself.

"What do you need help with?" he asked, stumbling into the kitchen while rubbing the sleep from his eyes. They normally didn't need to open till eight fifteen AM, about half an hour before school started. It was fortunate they had the breakfast club at school or most days he wouldn't have gotten breakfast at all.

"This," Arren said, she pushed a little clock in front of him. It looked like something from Ms Garibaldi's yard.

"What about it?" Chase asked.

"I cannot open it. I'm trying to get four point nine meters of copper wire so that I can repair my... my ship," she explained.

"Oh." Chase nodded. That made sense. "I think there's a screwdriver in Dad's shed. Did you get that from Ms Garibaldi's place?" He asked.

"Who is that?" She replied, following him out.

"That's the crazy old Italian lady who owns that place where your ship landed, she–"

Suddenly Arren stopped, looking horrified.

"You mean this belongs to someone else!" She said, almost bursting into tears. "Oh no, no, I am not a thief, I did not know, I did not know!"

"Hey, it's alright!" Chase said, not really understanding what was upsetting her.

"No, no, no!" She said, tearing up. "It's not my fault, it's not my fault!"

"Well, if anyone asks you can tell them I took it." He smiled.

She looked horrified.

"You'd *lie*..."

"No, it's not like a *real* lie!" He said but it had set her off again. "Hey, don't worry, we'll take it back. It's not like she'd miss it."

Arren looked puzzled at his words and upset with herself. "But I thought it was a refuse facility. You Earthlings are always throwing away things you don't want. I thought I could use anything there."

"Yeah," Chase agreed, "That place is such a dump it's no wonder you mistook it for the tip."

He gave her an uncertain pat on the shoulder and she brightened. "I will pay it off her!" She announced, a brave smile shining through her concern.

"*Buy* it, you mean. Sure. Why not? We'll pop by on the way to school."

That seemed to cheer her up, then she looked surprised. "You mean... I can come to school? Also too?"

"What? Yeah, sure, come along, I don't think anyone will mind."

She was almost trembling with excitement. "I have never been to school before! But you will not, I mean, won't tell them I'm from... far away?"

"Don't worry, I can keep a secret." Chase smiled.

She looked serious. "But don't lie either," she ordered.

"Sure," he agreed, not sure how it was possible to keep that kind of promise. Arren *was* hiding, that much was obvious. But what she was hiding from was still a mystery, one that Chase was unsure he wanted to know about. He reasoned that whoever she was hiding from it was worth the effort of keeping it a secret. One thing he did decide, however, was that he sure hoped nothing, or no one, would give her away.

She had them all organised so early that day that Chase and Lucky went to school at seven, via Ms Garibaldi's. As it was, Arren seemed to have a remarkable way with Ms Garibaldi as well. Chase and Lucky had to wait almost two hours listening to Ms Garibaldi's faltering English. They *tried* to be interested, but Arren sat there enthralled at every story, seeming to understand every word. Just as it was getting late, she suddenly burst into what sounded like perfect Italian and made some sort of request of Ms

Garibaldi, which she seemed to agree to instantly. After many kisses and too many hugs, she sent them on their way to school.

"Wow, that was weird. What kind of spell do you keep using on grown-ups?" Lucky asked. "I want some."

"It's not a spell, silly," she teased him, looking just a little cautious, like she didn't know if he was joking or not. "You just need to listen to them and they'll think very highly of you."

"Really?" Lucky said, probably planning some new chaos.

"Yes. I told her we need the space to do our homeworks for school," Arren explained. "And she promised to let us use some of the material in her yard if we ask first and clean as we go, polishing the knickknacks and the whatnots. It will be quite fun!"

"Sounds like work…" Lucky muttered.

***

The next three days were pretty weird. Arren went along to school and seemed to really enjoy trying to fit in, dressed in a mix of theirs and their mum's old clothes. No one appeared to doubt the story Lucky told them about her being an exchange student from France and all, especially since she now spoke French too. Dad had rung ahead and told the school that she was staying with him and even promised to send the paperwork as soon as he 'found' it again. So for the time being no one seemed to mind having her around.

Then, every afternoon right after school, Arren would rush them down to Ms Garibaldi's place and potter around at full speed. It was pretty obvious that they were not the only ones busy at this task because the trash yard seemed to be cleaning itself. They would all stay there until dark, when Lucky would pull them away from their plundering for a brief sleep and Arren would be up before dawn to work on things again.

Chase watched in wonder as Arren turned countless pieces of junk into useful things again and again. She mended an ornate kettle using pieces of an old toaster, and got a pair of BBQs going again with nothing more than an old hot water heater. She even fixed a dozen little watches by hand while talking to Ms Garibaldi. She usually wouldn't tell them what she was doing, just sent them on errands; 'find a toaster', 'find a flat screwdriver, 'bring the old oven from over there'. Then she'd get right back to work.

Arren was hard working, and seemed curious about everything. Chase noticed she had a very playful, almost cheeky personality. By the third day she'd gone so far as to arrange the junk in Ms Garibaldi's yard into a makeshift shed, cleverly disguised with rubbish to look like everything else. It seemed like Ms Garibaldi was never the wiser, Chase figured that she never toured her own rubbish tip anyway. Yet it wasn't until the end of the third day that Arren actually invited them inside.

Inside, Chase thought the shed looked *amazing*; it was not only useful, it was beautiful. Mechanical arms moved about on their own, enhanced by weird alien devices, pulling things apart and putting things together. A dozen knee high spider-like robots went about their business and the air inside was surprisingly fresh[3].

---

[3] Fresh air doesn't have too much pollution in it. So what is <u>air</u> made out of? Well, if air was split into five parts, four parts would be Nitrogen gas (fairly safe, it goes into your body, comes out again, doesn't usually do too much). One part would be oxygen gas (very important for staying alive). And then there's a tiny little bit of

Arren was welding something with an arc welder that she'd somehow built from an old fridge and broken car. She stopped and smiled at them. "Hello there, strangers," she joked. "It's not much but it worked. Here is my world!" She indicated at the shed.

There was some kind of machine, like an adapted evaporative air conditioner, except the air that was coming out of it smelt wonderful. The lights near the ceiling were glowing balls of electricity.

"How did you...?" Chase wondered, looking at the lights. He desperately wanted to know. An invention like that could be useful all over the world where poor people needed free, safe, wireless, floating lighting. An invention like that could make his family rich.

She looked up and sighed, seeming to know what he was thinking.

"I cannot tell you."

"Why not?" Lucky asked, sounding curious.

She looked at him. "Your people aren't ready. Your world has not yet created the understanding that leads to the glowing balls of light and if I told you it would be worse than cheating. I mean, for one, you could use this information to develop technologies that would destroy your planet, or mine. Your people aren't ready and when they are, they will discover this knowledge all on their own. To tell you before then would be a terrible crime, and if I told one of you the others would begin to think about the

---

everything else (dust, germs dead skin cells, pollen, argon, water vapour, carbon dioxide gas and a whole bunch of other things). Clean air isn't empty, it just has more of the stuff we want and less of the stuff we don't want, like germs and dust.

science unconsciously[4]. It's how it happens. You're just not ready for this kind of knowledge, you could destroy yourselves."

"So you've got all this science?" Lucky asked. "But you're not going to share any of it."

"But you've achieved so much for yourselves already!" She argued, sounding enthusiastic. "You can travel to your moon, you can read your DNA, more or less, you can cure world starvation if you choose to. When you're ready, you'll realise how."

Lucky scoffed.

"What do you think your people would do if they got their hands on my technology?" She asked him.

Lucky shrugged.

"What if we declared world peace?" Chase wondered. "Would your people share their science with us?"

"Gladly," she replied, "But over half the alien arrivals on your planet are killed and always have been. The last official embassy from the Universal Unity, back in 1947 to America, was damaged on entry[5]. Your people cut their bodies to shreds and tore their ship apart, losing most of its technology. The Unity, that's the Universal Unity, had to legally require the ship returned. But it sparked off many modern advances, like integrated circuits. So I'm sure that

---

[4] The existence of a collective unconscious mind (originally proposed by psychoanalyst Carl Jung) and expressed by such ideas as Rupert Sheldrake's "Morphic field" is not established in science. I'm using it here simply as a story tool to help explain why Arren can't tell them super advanced science secrets.

[5] I refer, of course, to the Roswell (New Mexico, USA) UFO incident – from whence springs the classic alien conspiracy theory that governments know about alien life but are covering up the information for reasons of their own, first published by Charles Fort in 1919. Probably false, but it does make a great story!

until your world meets Unity standards of peace and equality, it's not going to happen. But if you ask me, it's just never going to happen... at least not any time soon."

"Seems a dim view of our world," Lucky said.

"You Earthlings just seem to like it that way," she replied in a matter-of-fact way.

***

That night when they all got home, just as they walked through the front doors laughing, they found two tall men in dark suits talking to their dad. Chase's heart leapt in his chest.

The men were smiling, very friendly like, almost... too friendly like.

"Hey boys," one of them said with a big smile.

"Hey sons, hey Arren. These are Mr Flannigan and Mr Costa. They're from the Federal Police, apparently," Dad said in a very serious voice.

Everyone just stood there. The tall men didn't move, just stayed, there smiling and silent.

Dad moved himself to stand protectively next to them.

"Here're my boys and our exchange student, Arren. Say hi guys."

"Hi," they chorused, even Arren.

One of the tall men moved to shake their hands. Lucky and Chase didn't move but Arren did, shaking his hand in a very social manner. The man glanced over at Chase with a dark look.

"Now boys," Dad was saying, "Don't be so cold. These folks here just want to know if you know anything about a meteorite hitting the ground around these parts a few days ago. You don't know anything about that, do you?"

He looked at them like he was warning them to keep their secret.

"No," they chorused.

"I am sure a meteorite did not hit the ground a few days ago," Arren said with confidence. Chase realised she was telling the absolute truth but it was probably exactly what the strange men wanted to hear.

"That's nice to know," Officer Costa said, "Because if something did fall from outer space, it is legally the property of the Australian government."[6]

"Yeah," said Mr Flannigan, the one who liked to shake hands. "It could be, like, a *spy satellite*." He waved his hands dramatically.

Costa looked at him like he was an idiot.

"If you kids did see anything, you'll let us know?" Costa said in a not-too-friendly voice.

"Sure," said Chase.

"OK," said Lucky.

Arren said absolutely nothing.

Costa suddenly looked very dangerous. "This one," he said, pointing at Arren.

Flannigan whipped out a small, black, pointed device from his suit coat.

Arren gasped and stared at it.

"Now hang on there a minute!" Dad protested, interposing himself between them and the police. Costa was on him in a second, pushing him aside quite easily while keeping his eyes on them. Costa must have been very well built under his suit, he spoke to Dad in a professional voice but there was a definite threat in his tone.

---

[6] A slight exaggeration by Costa but still mostly true, see "protection of movable cultural heritage act 1986".

"Now there sir, no need to get all worked up. We are Federal Police, after all."

"If you harm the children..." Dad stuttered, voice catching, though he tried to sound brave.

"Nothing like that sir," Flannigan stated. "Just a simple scanning device, that's all," he said in a cheery voice. He pointed it at Arren then turned to Costa and shook his head no.

Costa did not look pleased. "Try the boys," he ordered.

Dad struggled, but Costa was a pro. He held him back and stared him down in a second.

"Nothing, again," Flannigan replied.

Costa cursed then looked at Dad all pleasant like. "There you go sir. No need to get all worked up. Nothing to be worried about here."

Dad pushed him away but then smiled a pleasant smile too, though he probably wasn't feeling it. He offered his hand but his voice was dark as he said, "Well then Mr Costa and Mr Flannigan, if your work here is finished, I'd like to offer my kids some dinner."

They smiled and shook Dads hand. Flannigan seemed all pleased and cheery but Costa took a good long look at Arren and said nothing. After they'd gone out they sat in their car for a long time, but eventually drove off.

As soon as they were gone, Dad looked serious.

"OK kids, what's really going on here? You've run away, haven't you Arren?"

She looked sad, like she was about to cry.

"I'm sorry, Mr Chase-and-Lucky's father." She stormed back and forth, looking more and more anxious. She muttered something in her native language. Suddenly she dashed into the kitchen and returned with a can of old soup.

"May I have this please?"

Dad looked at her seriously.

"Now dear, you can't run away from whatever this is forever. You'll have to confront it eventually. Stay here, we'll help you through-"

"No!" She said in a determined voice, then muttered to herself again, "You are too kind and innocent. This is not the sort of enemy you have any preparation against. I am sorry, I have brought strife to your family. I have brought strife to your world. I will leave right now," she said and whacking the can down on the table, stormed out.

"Wait!" Dad said, and she stopped short. He tossed her the can. Then reached behind the door and pulled out a backpack.

"This is for you," he said, handing it to her. She looked shocked. She stared at the bag and without opening it stated, "Change of clothes, food for three days, money. Mr Chase-and-Lucky's father!"

"Just call me Dad."

She smiled, then with a sad look started to walk briskly away.

Chase's heart was in his throat. Something about this scene was wrong.

"Dad, you can't just let her go like this."

He looked down at him, right down at him.

"I know," he said and pulled two more backpacks from behind the door. "I… just… had a feeling…" he muttered a weak explanation.

Chase and Lucky just looked at each other. For once their father's weirdness might have actually paid off.

"Be back in a week," he instructed them, "and keep her safe. Make sure she gets home. I'm going to grandma's for a while, should throw those government boys off your trail.

You know, I don't think they really are Federal Police, more like ASIO[7] or some other secret organisation. There's a conspiracy here, I can just *feel* it!"

For a brief moment, just for one moment, Chase wondered who was more insane; the father sending his young boys away for a week to help a girl get home, or the boys chasing an alien girl to who-knew-where.

Then the thought crossed his mind about how well his father had prepared, as if he'd known it was coming all along, and he wondered if maybe his dad was actually the sanest person in the world.

Chase didn't have any time to wonder about it, Arren was walking away at incredible speed. They had to run to catch up and jog to keep up.

"Arren, wait, we're coming!" He said almost out of breath.

"No!" She insisted.

"We're coming anyway," Lucky replied.

She stopped. "That device. *That is why we keep secrets from the Earthlings!* It's a kind of matter detector but it can tell if materials are produced off world. I had to break it. It's very simple but the technology can be adapted to make some terrible weapons. Localised earthquakes, teleporting organs out of someone's body. Just the kind of weapons your governments would *love* to get their hands on. What do you think I do all night? Sleep? No, I 'surf' your internet. I find out the news the rest of you ignore. I read the patterns in history and in your politics. Do you even know what your own people are knowingly allowing to happen on your world?" She started to storm off again.

"Umm," Chase muttered.

---

[7] The <u>Australian Security and Intelligence Organisation</u>, Australia's version of the FBI in America.

"And *that* is why we keep secrets from the Earthlings!" She shouted again.

"Hey, we're not like that. We're coming with you!" Lucky argued.

"Yeah, we'll look after you," Chase said.

"You have no say in the matter, for you cannot come if I don't let–" She stopped shouting suddenly and gasped.

There, in front of them and just down the street, a mysterious green light was floating around.

She dashed behind some nearby bushes and they jumped in after her. She was just about to push them out again but the light began to float in their direction.

They fell silent. There was something instinctively evil about that little green light, and it carried with it an ambiance of fear that Chase had never before felt in his life.

"What is it?" He whispered.

She put her fingers to her lips and waited.

It was floating up the street towards them, bobbing backwards and forwards like it was trying to peek into things, like letter boxes and windows.

Arren closed her eyes and muttered something. For a moment Chase thought his vision had become fuzzy until he realised it was actually the air around them, shimmering like it does in a heat wave.

They waited with bated breath for the strange light to pass, and watched as it bobbed slowly and leisurely up the road. Just as it came near them, Chase felt a tremendous rush of fear that it would somehow find them.

And it stopped.

It seemed to sense fear, and Arren gave him a look of chagrin.

It was approaching, gliding slower and slower towards them. Suddenly Chase found himself utterly unable to move from the fear. His skin went completely dry and he felt terribly cold. He started shaking uncontrollably. He could not move. The light was getting closer and closer. He couldn't even scream.

Suddenly there was a gentle *whoosh* and a very loud *ping*. The green light rocketed back towards the far end of the street and collapsed in the gutter.

Lucky had hit it with a broken fence paling.

Arren was shocked. "You... you..." It seemed to be all she could say.

Lucky snuck over towards the fading light. Chase was still too terrified to speak and was surprised to find that at some point he'd started to hold Arren's hand. He dropped it as quick as he could.

"Weird," said Lucky, "Looks like a cross between a robot and a fairy."

"It's a Will-o," Arren explained, "Sent by my old owners, the Coebri; They're... they're like *pirates*. We have to go now. You have to go too. It has sensed you. They will hunt you too. You are no longer safe here," she said in deep concern to Chase.

"Where he goes, I go," Lucky said in determination.

"Very well," she agreed, which was a bit of a surprise. Chase didn't know whether to feel grateful, or worried.

Quick as they could, and in Arren's case that was very quick, they ran down to Ms Garibaldi's junkyard. It was fortunate that the moon was quite bright because it was very late.

"Where are we going to go?" Chase asked.

"We can try hiding out at Grandma's with Dad," Lucky suggested. He liked Grandma's.

"We need to leave Australia," Arren said.

"Why Australia?" Lucky asked.

"You heard that man!" Arren explained, getting angry. "If it falls from the sky in Australia it belongs to the Australian government. I cannot give the spaceship to your government, it would be a disaster for your world. I have to leave right now and break another law again. I cannot stay here any longer!"

"I don't get it," Lucky argued, "If they don't know where you're hiding, what's the big problem?"

"No, it is not all right!" Arren shouted. "Earthlings! How can you just simply break your own laws like that? Don't you know what it does to your … your… grrr, you don't even have a word for it yet!" She kicked the ground in frustration. "How about soul? Do you have any idea of the physics of what terrible damage a lie, or a broken law, can do to your soul?" She asked.

They didn't know.

"We're not all that bad!" Lucky claimed with a light hearted smile.

She didn't seem convinced.

"And now I have to take you with me," she said, seeming so very sorry. "Come on guys."

Carefully they let themselves into Arren's shed. She spoke a few commanding words in her own language and suddenly everything began to fall apart, lights raced together and disappeared inside the door of her spaceship.

"How are we all going to fit in there?" Lucky asked.

She smiled at him.

"It's not the ship, Lucky. It's just the door."

She went in, stepping on one edge of the door as though gravity took on a new direction inside; she was standing sideways as if down to her was now the bottom of her ship's door.

"Come on in gentlemen," she invited.

Lucky was in there in a second, stumbling into the strange device she called a door. She laughed and helped him through.

Chase looked around at what may well be his last sight of planet Earth. He was nervous, but Arren held out her hand to help him in.

"I will take care of you, too." She smiled.

Before he could disagree, Lucky's voice could be heard from inside the spaceship, "Cool! Check this out!"

With a big breath of crisp night air, Chase allowed himself to be led inside the spaceship, feeling the way gravity changed direction as he got in.

He did not see the pair of envious eyes watching him through a crack in the shed door. Beady, greedy, envious eyes…

Chapter 4
Leaving Earth

The entry room was round, big enough for a small house, and almost all white. The first thing Arren did was make them take a sonic shower, right then and there, clothes and all. There was a gentle breeze, then the air pressure warped, changing in weird directions like at a rock concert. It emitted strange sounds almost too diverse to imagine, but in their echoes every inch of dirt and dust fluttered away from his body and onto the floor. As soon as the noise switched off a bright, warm light shone from the roof. Arren sighed and breathed in deeply. It must have shone for only five seconds or so, but long before it had finished Chase discovered to his amazement that he was completely clean. His hands felt smooth, soft just like a baby's hands.

"Ahh, that's much better," Arren declared. "Well, come on in!"

The door slid open to reveal the interior of the spaceship. It was like the inside of Arren's shed, only much busier. Dozens of spider machines clattered over floors and ceilings, working hard. Many other half-insect robots were waiting around, looking like mining machines, in good nick, but otherwise ignored. The lighting was hundreds of those little glowing electricity balls Arren had used to light her shed. They seemed to move about wherever they thought they were most needed. However, unlike what Chase was used to imagining as super futuristic materials of metal and plastic, everything seemed to be made of a gentle, spongy white rubber, as if the whole inside of the ship was made to be a kid safety zone at the supermarket. Even the metals squished a bit when he pushed on them.

She led them down a corridor that was wide and sloped upwards, tall enough for a large adult to walk through. They passed by several rooms and storage areas, all immaculately clean.

"How big is it in here?" Lucky stared in amazement.

"As big as it needs to be," Arren replied. "But not too big, I just crammed the extra rooms into interdimensional space. I used to ship materials between asteroids, so I suppose there's quite a bit of room in here."

"Yea, about that." Lucky scowled, "I think, Arren... whatever-your-name-is, that you owe us a bit of an explanation."

She sighed. "Arrendrallendriania. Ok, but come to the control room first."

She led them down another corridor and into what might have been the control room. It was amazing, more like an observatory than a control room. The roof was filled with an image of the two hundred billion stars of the Milky Way[8], all in infinitely more detail than was possible on Earth. Chase found that the longer he looked, the more detail he could see among the stars. When he looked long enough he could even see planets orbiting distant suns.

"This is *amazing!*" Chase gasped in wonder.

Arren seemed pleased. She stepped up onto a little platform, taking a seat in what must be the pilot's chair. Chase liked it; it was a big plush burgundy armchair that swivelled freely in the air, probably held up by a cushion of magnetism or something. She seemed to be controlling the ship just by thought as there were no control panels visible.

Around the walls of the room dozens of screens floated around in mid-air displaying images from all over the

---

[8] And there are hundreds of billions of galaxies! The <u>Universe</u> is HUUUUUGE!

Earth, including one of the door of their craft still sitting on the ground.

"How do you get the pictures?" Chase asked.

"Scrying sensors; they put a hole in space and let the light shine through to here. Quite simple physics when you get the knack of it."

Chase *really* wished he had the knack of it, but somehow he didn't think his alien friend was about to tell him, especially with all the 'keeping secrets from the Earthlings' thing.

"Let's get out of here first," she said. Suddenly the image of their door shimmered and disappeared, leaving only a glowing green outline. This outline shifted, it looked like the now invisible ship was moving towards the door of the fallen shed. However, Chase and Lucky could feel nothing.

"We'll move slowly," she said.

"How are you bending the light around to make us invisible?" Chase asked.

"Well, most of the ship is in extra dimensional space, so it's like it's not even here. Except for the door, I can't shift the door into another dimension, it's too dangerous. But why go to all that effort to make the door invisible when I can simply require the light to not interact with its particles? Make them transparent, like glass. Microwaves are a bit difficult though, hopefully your scanners out at the airports won't pick us up as we fly around. But I've got a few tricks to deal with that too," she explained.

Chase was watching the screens, trying to take in every detail. He could have stayed there all day learning about advanced alien technologies, even if he wasn't *supposed* to.

"Well, this is all very fascinating," Lucky agreed, "But we still need some answers if we're going to help you."

"Yes, yes, I promised," she replied, stepping down from her chair. Using her hands, she spun the image on the ceiling until she found a teeny, tiny star somewhere far away in another galaxy.

"I come from there," she explained, a note of sadness to her tale. "I was born a slave. Now don't get me wrong, most of the universe is a great place, but once in a while, a world or two choose to rebel from the Universal Unity and live under their own laws."

"And the Unity lets them get away with it?" Lucky wondered.

"Of course," she replied, seeming confused. "The Unity is built on peace and understanding, they haven't had a battle in their entire history. They won't force anyone to do something they haven't chosen to! It's against the law!"

She made it sound like it was one of the most obvious things in the universe.

"I wish someone would tell our teachers that..." Lucky thought out loud.

Then she continued. "So, I am from one of the worlds, one of the civilisations actually, that refuses to work with the Universal Unity. I was made, well, born to work with this ship as its biologically melded pilot. It didn't matter that I could fly through space or talk or *feel!* They only wanted me to dig, and to move things from one place to another. And they were cruel to any who didn't work, I could have been executed. That... that's what it's like to be born on one of the Coebri worlds."

"Coebri worlds?" Chase asked.

"Yes, one of the cultures that rebelled many centuries ago from the Unity. They've been getting worse ever since."

"And the Universal Unity is pretty much everyone else?" Lucky pondered.

"Sort of... but there are still loads of independent worlds. The Unity world are usually very good, helpful, even obedient. They won't force anyone to join but they'll protect those that don't yet have a choice, like Earth. Everyone knows about Earth. It's unlike any other planet in the Cosmos; hypocritical, dishonest, inexplicably violent. You," she pointed at Lucky, "you even use violence for entertainment! I cannot believe you shoot people for fun... what... what kind of *monsters* ..."

She stuttered, seeming lost for words. Then she pulled herself together.

"Sheesh, it's just a computer game," Lucky said, crossing his arms. He didn't like her accusation. "Besides, there's something *I* don't get. If you got away from these Coebri, why don't you just go to the Unity for protection?"

"They won't," Chase realised.

"What?" Lucky asked.

"Don't you see? The Universal Unity won't recognise her as one of their own. They probably have laws against it, and I bet if she went to them they'd hand her right back to the Coebri," Chase explained.

Arren gave a smile of great relief. "Yes, that's right." She seemed very impressed. "I had to break a law. I had to break the Coebri law and flee from those... those pirates. I broke a law and the Universal Unity only knows laws. On Earth you make laws, but so many times the rules are twisted to serve the powerful. It's not like that in the rest of the universe, for the most part. Rules are good. Rules are based on true understanding, not petty grabs for power. Your people may not have realised that yet, but they will."

"Rules," Lucky scoffed, "were made to be broken!"

"Spoken like a true Earthling," Arren said with disgust.

"So," Chase said, trying to disarm things, "The universe is a pretty nice place when you don't break Unity laws."

"Almost all nice, but not the Coebri. They're terrible. Now they even go from world to world trying to get them to reject the Universal Unity too. They're here on Earth sometimes, when they manage to get past the blockades, or when they're invited by Earth leaders. It's very bad. I'm not sure how well Earth will do in the future if things don't improve," she said, and sighed.

"Is that why you tried to hide here?" Chase asked. "It isn't a pirate world and it isn't a Unity world."

"Plus, it's so violent and messy that only a fool would try hiding out here," she finished.

Chase and Lucky raised their eyebrows at each other.

"So... where do we go now?" Chase asked.

"Somewhere that doesn't have many laws..." she said.

"We could try Antarctica," Lucky said, "I don't think there are any laws there yet, it's not even a proper country."

"Oh, there are laws there, I checked that already. Though I suppose there are fewer people. We can stay there 'til I can get the quantum teleporter ready again. I burnt it out trying to escape the first time. Didn't really get a chance to line things up properly..." she regretted.

Suddenly Lucky screamed, "Snake!"

Chase looked around, a huge green boa constrictor slid along the floor towards Arren.

"Lopi!" Arren said in excitement. "Where have you been today?!"

"You... you have a pet snake?" Chase said, and stepped back. He looked at the massive python as it slithered up Arren's arm to lick at her affectionately. Then it turned its cold reptilian eyes towards him. It seemed to be saying, 'watch your back Earth-man, or I'll swallow you whole next time she's not looking!'

"Of course I have a snake. They are wonderful pets, very clever conversationalists," she said, jittering to it in her mysterious language. Then it actually seemed to hiss back a reply.

"No, they're friends, even if they *are* Earthlings," she replied in English, snuggling up to it. "Ooh, I've missed you today, who's a cutie, whoooo's a cutie!!"

"Space girl has a pet snake." Lucky rolled his eyes in disbelief.

"I wonder what other surprises are on this ship?" Chase said aloud.

Arren didn't answer him.

Neither did Lopi.

"So..." he said, wondering what would happen next.

A small beeping came from the ceiling and it suddenly shifted towards the normal night sky, except now a little red circle was flashing over near the Southern Cross.

Lopi dropped to the floor and Arren leapt onto her chair.

"A tracker!" She yelled. "Grab hold of something!"

Chase and Lucky clutched onto the padded banister around her control platform. She was concentrating hard and several images on the screen went into a wild spin. They showed the ship lifting violently up, several kilometres in a second, making a right-angled turn without slowing down and then free falling towards the earth.

"Did we just do a right-angled turn without slowing down?" Chase asked.

"Duh, alien technology!" Lucky said.

"No, seriously, how did we do that?"

"Independent inertial reference frame," Arren muttered.

"Oh I see," Chase said not really seeing at all.

"Oh, I see," Lucky mocked. "Hey, is it just me or are we falling towards the surface of the earth?"

"It's not just you, we're actually falling," Arren said.

"Umm, should we be worried?" Chase asked.

Arren didn't answer.

The ground was getting closer and closer as they fell faster and faster.

"Why isn't the air slowing us down?" Chase wondered.

"Terminal velocity[9] does not exist to a vehicle transparent to the matter of the air[10]," she muttered, concentrating hard. "I'm hiding our position, hoping the tracker will be thrown off and follow our last known direction."

And closer and closer.

"Arren..." Chase said, getting ever more worried.

Suddenly she looked up, "Oh yeah."

And the ship came to an instantaneous halt over a field of cows. One of them walked up without pausing, walking

---

[9] "Terminal velocity" is the speed at which you stop speeding up. Basically, falling towards earth is a pretty windy experience, wouldn't you agree? Well, at some point, the pull of gravity is balanced by the push of the wind. That is, the wind is so strong you don't speed up any more, even though you're still falling pretty fast - about 55 meters every second. It is terminal because you stop speeding up. Also at that speed you're still likely to die when you hit the ground, and so in that sense it's pretty 'terminal' too!

Parachutes make good use of this wind, using their size to greatly increase the resistance, helping to slow a fall.

[10] "Transparent to matter" means that Arren's ship is somehow 'magically' not interacting with nearby atoms, they're passing right on through as if the ship isn't actually there. Maybe they're simply out of phase? Not interacting with matter means there's no wind, and no wind means no terminal velocity – the ship will fall faster and faster and faster till it gets to the centre of the earth and flies right on through!

right through the same place the door was without seeming to notice it at all; it was like they were in a ghost ship now.

Arren sat back. "Good point Chase, he'll probably notice the wake in the aether[11] if we'd sliced through the denser matter of the surface of the earth."

"You mean we weren't going to crash?" He asked.

She looked surprised. "Of course not." Then she laughed. "What, you think this is my first time flying?"

They were quite relieved.

"I still can't believe your ship can be moving so much and we don't feel a thing," Chase said.

"Yeah, what happened to 'grab hold of something'?" Lucky agreed.

"Oh, it's a figure of speech I picked up from your science fiction shows. We're currently within an independent inertial reference frame. Basically it means the ship can move and go wherever it wants and we don't feel a thing. The ships interior is protected from any external change in speed or direction. It's only possible once you get the angular moments of every particle moving at speed of... I've ... said too much."

Chase was about to beg her to say more when the alarm went off again.

"Oordya! Didn't fool it," Arren sounded worried. Suddenly the ship took off and went into outer space.

"Oh no!" She sounded even more worried.

"What, what is it?"

---

[11] Ahh, aether, do you really exist? Look up 'Luminiferous aether' on Wikipedia. Light travels in waves, a lot like ocean waves travel through water. However, if ocean waves travel through water, what do light waves travel though? Scientists suspect they don't travel through anything, which is a pretty mysterious thing... Again I'm just using this idea to help tell a story.

"He's closing in. Well, you're an Earthling, arm yourself!" She shouted.

Lucky hoisted up his fence paling, which apparently he'd brought with him.

Arren stared at it in shock, perhaps regretting what she'd said. "No. He's got us, brace yourselves!"

This time they really did need bracing as the room suddenly jolted violently backwards and they were thrown forwards onto the reasonably soft floor, except Lucky, who managed to leave an impression of his face in the slowly reshaping metal bulkhead.

"Ouch," he said.

"What happened to our ultimate inertial reference-?" Chase began.

"Where is he, where is he?" Arren shouted in panic, brushing her clothes down wildly. The screens began to flash images of her ship, only this time they were looking right into the other dimension where the ship was hidden.

It was gigantic. A huge, misshapen, square based pyramid, as long as an Aussie rules football field and tall as a skyscraper. It was covered with a random collection of cubic rooms and twisting corridors. Antennae, landing platforms, mining lasers, solar cells and cranes all stuck out in random directions, the door on one side near the base. The whole place looked like it had been added to over the years with no thought given to the previous architecture or overall structure. It looked like a badly designed house with a million random extensions.

And there, on the side, was a silver man almost three meters tall. He was muscular like Superman, except he had glowing silver eyes. He reached out his arm towards them.

"There!" Chase shouted, pointing at him. "How does he survive in space?"

"How does he fly?" Lucky asked.

"Get him off, ouch!" Arren said.

Suddenly the silver man began to merge his hand with Arren's ship. Then he put his whole arm through. Images began to flicker and fade and Arren clutched her side and fell to the ground, her irises looking like they were cracking under the strain.

"No!" She said in pain.

Suddenly the silver man appeared on the main screen, covering the entire roof. He spoke and his voice sounded authoritative and passionless, like a machine.

"Arrendrallendriania," he said, "You are in breach of Coebri law, section code one five point nine three point one nine nine three eight five. As a lawful enforcer of the Universal Unity, I require you to return to your owner."

"Never," she said in a husky voice, holding her side like it hurt too much to get up. "He lied to me. I choose to live on Earth."

"Earth is not a recognised sanctuary world, neither do you have the permission of Earth's rulers to live in their world-"

Chase cut him off, "I am from Earth, and I claim this ship as my own!"

The silver man stopped. "You... you, young human male should not be riding in a class two reclamation and research vessel. It is in breach of Universal Unity law C nine point two point three three four – that Earth is under the veil of ignorance at this present date."

"So," Lucky yelled, "Let's just see you *try* to take her away!"

The machine looked unimpressed.

"Are you proposing to establish the validity of your claim through violence?" He asked.

"If we have to, you stupid, pompous..." Lucky shouted.

"Chase," Arren whispered.

"Yes?" He snapped.

"Arrogant, ignorant, foolish..." Lucky continued.

"Chase, do I have your permission to run away?" Arren writhed on the floor in pain, twisting to look at him with a desperate look in her eyes.

"Dumb, stupid, snotty..."

"Chase, do I have your permission to run away?" She repeated.

Chase had no idea what this meant, or why she wanted his permission but he suspected that he didn't have the time to find out.

"Loudmouthed, blind, ignorant, oh wait, I already said that..."

"Yes...?" Chase shrugged.

Arren screamed like she was pulling out a splitter and the silver man looked at her in alarm.

"Child, do not–"

He didn't finish. Suddenly Arren's spaceship exploded from the side, ripping the silver man's arm off in the process. She kept on screaming and crying in pain for at least five minutes. Lopi slithered up and tried to comfort her but she was doubled over and wouldn't move. The silver man was nowhere to be seen and outside the stars were all different and very few. They'd moved somewhere, quickly and very violently.

Chase didn't know what to do, there seemed to be nothing he could do to help her.

"Arren... Arren..." He kept on saying, but she just grabbed his hand and held on tight.

After the screaming died down, Lucky stood up. "I think I'll go and check out what just happened."

Lopi slithered out and stood in his way.

"Ahh," he said, holding his fence paling dangerously.

"Don't," Chase said, "I think she's trying to help."

Lopi slithered to the door and turned around to look at him.

"Can't you Earthlings speak to animals yet?" Arren smiled in wry humour, still clutching herself in pain.

Lucky carefully laid his fence paling down on the control deck floor, then he grinned and followed the snake out.

He was back in ten minutes. Arren was curled up in her chair, Chase patting her hand.

"That snake sure knows her way around your ship," Lucky said, sitting down and sighing. "You blasted a hole in the side. There's a huge chunk of spaceship just floating out there in space, I saw it out the window. All the decks are torn up and there are wires and junk just floating out there."

"That's a relief," Arren said, looking pale. "I thought we'd lost my side for good."

"Can you fix it?" Chase asked.

"Not from here," she replied. "I need to go out there and cut off the tracker's arm. It'll reactivate unless we do."

"What *was* that tracker?" Lucky asked.

"A sub-sentient machine, self-aware, but not alive. Just really, really complex. Not like me. I am alive," she explained, somewhat cryptically.

"Ahh... Arren, I don't think you're in any shape to get up and fix your ship," Chase said.

"You do it," she offered, looking at him with hope filled eyes. "You own this ship now. At least, for now. We're outside Unity law. Well, for as long as you can hold on to me. To me and this ship I mean, I'll be safe," she explained.

"You want me to go out and fix the ship?" He said.

She nodded, smiling a delicate smile laced with hope.

"Ok..." He agreed, unsure of how he'd begin.

"Wait, Arren, why don't you just use some sort of gravity beam and pull the bit back in?" Lucky said.

"I will, once the arm is out. But then you'll need to suture the wound back together. Do you get it Chase? You need to cut out the arm then sew up the wound."

"Ahh, how do I do that?" He asked.

"Oh, that's right, you're an Earthling," she said, sounding disappointed.

She began crawling towards the exit. Chase helped her up and supported her as she walked. She was in incredible pain.

"Why are you hurt?" Chase finally asked.

She answered as she stumbled down the hallway, leaning on him. "This ship and I are connected. I can feel it like it's a part of my own body."

"You mean you can feel anything this ship touches," Chase asked.

"Yes, just like that."

"How? Do your nerves somehow run though this entire ship?"

"Something like that."

"And when the ship hurts, you hurt."

"Exactly."

Chase said nothing. He was just plain angry. He imagined the Coebri making her dig through solid rock using her own hands as a drill. No wonder she had to escape.

They went past the main room to the little entry room. Even the spiders seemed to share her pain, sitting there all curled up or limping slowly around.

"Now, the hull of the ship is metal, right?" Arren explained through her pain. "So, like all metals, it is more easily malleable by thought. You can shape it using your own... imagination, right?"

"I thought you weren't supposed to tell us anything Earthlings didn't already know?" Lucky teased her, trying to make light of the very serious situation they were in.

"What makes you think your people don't already know this[12]?" She asked him rhetorically.

He shut up.

"Here, you can put these headbands on. You can use them to communicate with me and they should help you reshape metals without any training. And you'll need these spacesuits," she said.

The headbands were silver, but heavy like stone, and were set with intricate lines and delicate circuitry. The spacesuits, however, looked like full body swimsuits with fishbowls for helmets, complete with skin-tight gloves and gravity boots.

---

[12] A dose of parapsychology: can metals really be reshaped by thought? Uri Geller certainly thought so. Scientists, however, are not so sure...

"We need these to breathe right?" Lucky offered, looking at the bowls.

She looked surprised.

"Yes, and to prevent explosive decompression. Do you know, Lucky, what would happen to you if you stepped outside a spaceship with only the helmet on?"

"Ahh, you'd freeze to death?"

"Only in the shadows. In the sun you'd bake like a chicken in a hot oven in only seconds. Without the air to protect you, you'd die pretty quick in space. But it's not the heat or cold that would kill you first…"

She was leaning forward, telling her gory story with glee. She seemed to be getting a bit morbid in her agony.

"…but the decompression. Liquids are just gasses under pressure. Without air pressing all around you, like it is on Earth, all the liquids in your body would turn into gas and boil away in seconds. You cannot see air pressure, or even feel it, unless it changes suddenly. But air pressure keeps you alive all the time without any effort on your part. Go out there without something pressing in on every square centimetre of your body and the result would be an explosion beginning with your *eyeballs*. [13]"

"That's gross," Lucky protested.

She whispered like she was telling him a dreadful secret, "Did you know that you cannot even suck air in? You just make a gap in your body and the nearby air pressure pushes the air in. You don't even *earn* your own breath…"

"Ahh, do you want us to go out and fix your ship or not?" Lucky asked.

She nodded, looking a little pale.

---

[13] Air pressure is amazing! See my video for an explanation at www.drjoe.id.au.

They put the suits on, assuming Coebri once wore them to help mine asteroids. They had to strip almost completely naked, so Lopi and Arren waited outside while they changed in the entry room. She explained that the suits acted like air pressure on Earth, pressing in on them and kept their bodies' liquids from exploding out of them. The air in their helmets kept their eyes from doing the same thing, and let them breath. A cleverly engineered moss in the narrow backpack filtered their air and Arren assured them that they would starve to death before they ran out of clean air to breathe.

Chase found that fact only moderately reassuring.

"Make sure you don't forget which way is down," she said. She smiled a weak smile from the screen, turned off the gravity in the entry room and let all the air hiss out.

For a brief moment Chase forgot to worry, he was floating in space! It was unlike anything he'd ever felt before and thought it so wonderful that he knew *exactly* what he wanted to do with his weekends for the rest of his life – float. Simply float around space.

"OK boys!" Arren's voice cut through his playtime, speaking telepathically to them through the headbands. "Use the subjective directional gravity[14] in your boots to walk on out."

They left through the door they had come in, seeing in person for the first time just how massive Arren's class two research and reclamation vessel was. The size of the space ship was *amazing*.

"Well, we'd better get to work," Lucky said, pointing towards the back of the craft.

---

[14] These make believe boots let you choose which way is down – very useful when floating in space! They also make the local gravity feel just right for you.

Chase gasped.

"What, what is it?" Arren said.

The damage was immense. Along one side, a whole third of the hull was floating out in space, a rough chunk at least fifty meters long. Between it and the ship a junkyard of debris floated. On the rest of the ship mysterious, floating sheets of white cloth seemed to be preventing anything else from flying out.

To be honest, the whole situation looked irreparable.

"What? What?" Arren repeated.

"It's OK," Chase lied, "We'll have it patched up in a second."

"It's bad, isn't it? All my external sensors are down, thanks to that tracker!"

"Naaa," Lucky lied too, "Not bad at all!"

"Hmm. Can you see the arm? You just need to cut out the arm, I can do the rest."

"Let's get a bit closer to the missing section," Chase said. They walked up the side of the ship, not at all slow like the spacemen on TV. To Chase it was more like taking a walk in the park, or even easier.

"There's no air to slow us down," Chase said to Lucky, "I'm glad we don't have to wear those heavy NASA space suits. I hear they weigh over a hundred kilos. These suits are, what two or three kilos?"

"Yeah, look, I can dance!" Lucky boasted, shuffling around.

"Do I need to remind you of what you're doing out there!" Arren yelled.

For a peace-loving alien she could be awfully forceful, Chase thought.

They came to the section where the side had been blasted out and looked around.

"There it is," Lucky said, pointing.

Chase could see an arm half sticking into the inside of the ship.

"How do we get over there?" He asked.

"Jump?" Lucky suggested.

"Subjective directional gravity!" Arren yelled. "Just point the stupid boots where you want to go and imagine that way is down!"

She sure seemed anxious.

"You all right there?" Lucky asked.

"Yeah, fine, just ... do what you need to do," she said a bit quieter.

The boys looked at each other.

"All right, calm down *princess*. We're on our way!" Lucky said with a cheeky smile.

There was only one conclusion, Chase reasoned, Lucky *liked* teasing Arren.

Chase was the first to work out how to do it. He lay on his back and pointed his feet at the floating mass, then convinced himself that down was now towards the missing part of the space ship and drifted towards it gently. Lucky took a lot longer and in the end had to jump first and turn around in mid-flight. It seemed a lot harder for him to turn around in space without anything dense like air to push off from. He had to spin his arms in circles one way to slowly convince his body to spin the other way. He almost landed face first but the boots took over at the last moment and he hit just right.

Chase began to try to mentally cut the arm out of the side of the ship. It was a lot harder than it sounded to psychokinetically[15] reshape metal using alien enhancement

---

[15] Psychokinesis is the ability to move things by thought, without touching them. It is also called telekinesis. Again, science has not

devices. They tried to cut a nice circle in the metal around the embedded arm but kept smudging and smearing the metal instead. In the end, Lucky told Chase to go around the other side so they could work on it from both angles.

He agreed with some reluctance. While walking around the ship's broken hull, he had to convince himself that down was up again and he ended up walking on the outside of the floating bulk. He noticed then that it was turning ever so slowly from when they first jumped on it. He hoped that would not cause a problem when they wanted to get off.

The arm, it was sad to see, looked like it had been violently torn from its socket, silver mechanical ligaments and bones split and splintered. He hoped that sub-sentient life forms didn't feel real pain, like Arren did.

They worked on it for a good ten minutes before they finally smudged and smeared it enough to break through. Arren was coaching them, but it was hard work.

"Stop thinking metal is so solid, it's responding to your thoughts!" She finally screamed in frustration, "Picture it like water, watch it *flow* away from the arm."

"We're trying!" Lucky shouted.

"Keep trying," she whispered, her voice suddenly sounding very weak.

"Arren, Arren! Are you all right?" Chase said in alarm. Lucky stopped.

"Sure," she said dreamily, "It's just, I never realised it's so quiet out here..."

"Arren no! Wake up!" Lucky shouted. "Don't go to sleep, tell us how to fix the ship again."

---

found convincing proof that it exists, or how it would work if it did. What would you do if you were psychokinetic?

"... fix the ship..." She said in a fading voice. "It's so hard, so hard to always fight. I need a good, long... slee–" they heard a thump as she fell to the ground.

"Arren, no!" Chase shouted.

"Bro, get back," Lucky roared. Suddenly, he kicked the arm with all his force. The metal buckled but held fast. Chase heard him cursing as he limped around.

"Do it again!" Chase insisted. He bent down, touching his helmet to the bulkhead. He was worried about Arren, he was worried for himself, and he was worried for his dad. He looked at the metal stubbornly doing what it was made to do, holding onto the severed alien robot arm.

No, not stubbornly. Weakly. Like water, just dripping away. Drip, drip.

Smash.

Lucky's foot hit with great force and the arm blasted away, drips of metal disappearing into space.

Without waiting another moment Chase began to imagine the metals flowing together. Something must have happened inside him because the wound in the hull began to close immediately, lining itself in seconds.

"Dude, you did it!" Lucky cheered.

"Yeah, I–" Chase began, then he realised he was no longer touching the hull. It was drifting slowly back towards the rest of the ship, leaving him floating out in space.

"...what's going on?!" Chase said in alarm.

"The broken piece is moving back in, I can't, ah, it's pushing me back in too!" Lucky said.

"I'm stuck out here!" Chase shouted, then he remembered his gravity boots.

"The boots!" Lucky said at the same time.

Great minds... Chase laughed to himself.

Suddenly his boots gave a suspicious click. A green flash of light appeared nearby, but he didn't get a proper look at it and wasn't even sure he'd seen it. But the boots had stopped working.

Something was wrong.

"Lucky, Lucky!" He shouted in fear.

But there was no answer.

The headband had stopped working too. Perhaps he'd overdone it trying to repair Arren's ship? The broken hull was slowly sliding back into place like a jigsaw puzzle.

And Chase was floating away from the ship, bit by bit. Further and further away.

Arren was unconscious, his brother nowhere to be seen, it could be days before they found him again floating through the endless vacuum of space. It could be never. Unless he perhaps took off the helmet... it'd be a quicker way to...

There has to be a way out of this!

Chase didn't want to be floating around anymore, and promised himself he'd get back on board quick as possible. Looking around he saw a bottle amid the rubble floating free from Arren's ship. A simple bottle filled with liquid. It looked like the bottle he'd used for his rocket, screw lid and all. It seemed ironic that for thousands of years of technological evolution the simplest and most effective lid might still be a screw top.

He stretched out, only just grabbing the bottle by the neck as it spun slowly around in the gravity-less void.

Now, how to use this to get out of here? He wondered[16].

For a brief moment he thought about throwing the bottle at the ship to let them know he was still out here, but then

---

[16] Any ideas...? ☺

he realised the force of throwing the bottle would also push him further away. 'Every action has an equal and opposite reaction', he recalled from Newton's something or other law[17]. So maybe if he threw the bottle *away* from the ship then he would float gently back towards it.

It was his safest option, but as he hefted the bottle in his hands it felt like it was only about two kilos[18]. Even if he threw it with all his might, he would float back very slowly. If only there was some way to increase the force...

He looked inside the bottle at the clear liquid. Probably water. Hopefully water and not flesh eating acid or something important. Some kind of liquid...

... and liquids, Arren has said, were just gasses under pressure.

And pressure meant force!

He placed the bottom of the bottle up against his stomach, near his centre of mass[19]. Then he turned around to face away from the ship, yet he continued to drift, making it almost impossible to keep his back exactly facing the spaceship. As quick as he could he unscrewed the bottle. It was a bit jammed at first, then some liquid squirted out from the edge of the lid, splattering his helmet and making it difficult to see. Whatever it was, it was very, very cold! Or maybe it became cold as it pressed out of the bottle and into the emptiness of space. The remaining gas rocketed off in all directions.

---

[17] <u>Newton's</u> Third Law.

[18] Let me just clarify, things still have mass in space, even if they don't weigh anything. Chase can tell if a bottle is about two kilos if he hefts it a bit.

[19] Your <u>centre of mass</u> is your balancing point, somewhere near your middle. It's not a physical point, more of a mathematical one.

Suddenly the lid popped right off the bottle, just like it did on his bottle rocket. The liquid squirted away from him with enormous pressure, vaporising almost instantly, shoving the bottle painfully into his stomach. Crystals of ice formed against the sides of the bottle as the remaining liquid froze.

Sure enough, the large acceleration of the small amount of liquid as it squirted away was enough to cause his body to move towards the ship, and in a little under a minute he was touching the ship again. Grabbing a hold of some pipes, he tapped on the hull.

A moment later, Lucky emerged and walked along the hull till he grabbed Chase's ankle. Then, with all the dignity of a bobbing helium balloon, Lucky dragged him along till they were both safely back inside the ship.

Then they raced to see Arren. It was dark inside now, the lights glowed dim and regretful, not moving at all. All the spider robots were motionless. Arren was back in the control room but she did not look good. She was collapsed on the floor, her face was pale and hair matted.

"Looks like ripping part off the ship has really hurt her," Chase said, cradling her head.

"You don't suppose she's not really human?" Lucky suddenly wondered.

"Of course she is, she's just biologically connected to this ship. She was a slave, remember?" Chase defended her.

"Yeah, be careful brother. Don't get messed up in her business," Lucky whispered.

Chase didn't tell him, but that's what his father had said too. For all his playfulness and teasing, there was a pretty sensible side to his crazy twin.

"There has to be some kind of medical room," Chase said.

Lopi hissed.

"I think the snake wants us to follow her. What is it, Snaky?" Lucky joked.

"This is serious!" Chase shouted. "She could die. I almost died. We could probably all go to jail…"

"I know," Lucky said in his rarely heard sombre voice, "I know. Come on, I'll help you carry her."

They did their best, slinging an arm over each shoulder and dragging her along. The snake, Lopi, lead them down several corridors, but never any stairs, until they came to a plain room with a single bed. But what a bed! It was covered with a glass dome and innumerable wires and tubes that ran between the floor and roof, running in, through and around about the bed.

Lopi slithered in and indicated towards the bed with her nose.

"I guess we put her on the bed," Chase surmised.

They dragged Arren over and lay her down. The glass dome slithered down and wires began detaching and attaching themselves from her body, focusing on her head and her side. Meanwhile, Lopi slithered confidently among them, pushing buttons, switching levers and gently rubbing Arren with her nose.

After ten minutes of the amazing scene, Lucky got bored. "You think we should leave them to it?" He asked.

"Yeah, I'm going to the bridge."

"You do that Chase, I'm going to take a look around again."

"I wouldn't go touching anything," Chase warned him.

"Me? Oh come on!" He said and danced out.

After watching for another minute Chase slowly left too, trying to ignore the giant boa constrictor staring at him, like he was supposed to do or say something… but didn't know what it was…

Chapter 5
The garden

Chase was sitting in the pilot's chair, watching the starry ceiling, when he finally heard Arren approaching. It must have been midnight back home on Earth. Midnight Wednesday. She hobbled into the control room wearing a shimmering light blue blanket and using a short rod as a walking stick.

"Hey, you're up!" Chase said, clapping his hands. He stood up as quick as he could to offer her the chair.

"Yes, thank you. Thank you for fixing things." She smiled.

Chase helped her sit down. She still seemed pretty sore.

"You gonna be alright?" He asked, concerned.

"Yes, eventually. Lopi is a master."

"Yeah, what was she doing?" Chase asked.

"Healing. Snakes make excellent healers. I don't know why you Earthlings haven't worked that out yet. Actually, you know many of your ambulances still have images of snakes. Do you know why? Did you know that? Huh, huh!" She teased in a soft voice[20].

He'd never heard that, no. But still, she seemed so unwell. "What happened to you?"

"Have you heard of wormholes?"

"Yes, a hole through space," he said.

"Not quite. Joining two points of space with a micro singularity[21] is a bit closer to the mark. I created a

---

[20] I'm not giving that away, but it's called the 'Caduceus' or 'rod of Asclepius' for your own reference. Can snakes heal? Again, this is used as a story device.

[21] AKA a very small black hole.

wormhole and threw myself into it, making sure the tracker was outside the event horizon at the time. Sadly, he was still connected to the hull, but outside, so we tore each other apart. I'm neurologically connected to the hull, it hurt like having my own side torn out."

"That sounds terrible,' Chase sympathised.

"It was worth it," she said with an ironic smile.

"Do you… think he died?" Chase asked.

"Oh, don't worry. He's a sub-sentient organism; a complicated computer. They'll repair him, if they can."

"Oh, that's good. A complicated computer that can fly through outer space and merge with alien spaceships," he said, still worried.

"Yes, but you're *human*," she argued. Chase wondered what she meant and why that would be important, but let the matter drop.

"What do you think we should do now?" He asked.

"I don't know," she replied, sighing as she sat back and shut her eyes.

After a moment of silence he asked her. "What was it like, working for the Coebri?"

She paused, looking over her star covered ceiling. "Dark. Always dark. And very cold. I never saw a sun, it was so far away from the asteroid belt it just looked like a big star. And the Coebri never spoke to me, except to order me around. And whenever I did something they didn't like, they'd give me electric shocks."

"That's insane!" He protested.

"But that wasn't the worst of it. They had a leader, my… father, of a sort. Tzaarkh. A tyrant. You might think him a corrupt business tycoon, or organised crime boss. Vengeful, dishonest. He would swindle anyone out of their own home, or world. He wouldn't stoop to murder, that's more of an

Earth thing. But he'd get people so in debt that he'd sell their own family as slaves. And he was merciless to those he considered his enemies."

"That sounds awful, no wonder you ran away," he said.

She smiled. "Oh, it wasn't all bad. I had Lopi, and my other pets. And I could read about faraway places. And I had a job to do; I didn't get bored, even though I didn't really get to rest properly either. It's how I learnt how to get by on two hours of sleep a night."

It made Chase feel so angry, but Arren patted his hand.

"Don't worry, I've put that all behind me."

"You know?" Lucky's voice chimed out from behind them, "I think this ship just keeps getting bigger every time I look around!"

Chase jumped, he hadn't heard his brother come in. Lucky looked at Chase with an 'I've got my eye on you' look, and Chase pulled his hand away from Arren's as quick as he could. He didn't want anyone to think he was holding a girl's hand, especially one from outer space.

"You know," Lucky continued, "This ship even has a garden, with a pool!"

"Of course, how else do you think I recycle all the air and food?" Arren said.

"Ahh, Lucky, you didn't take a drink in the pool did you?" Chase said, getting worried about how effective the water recycling process was.

"Why not? I use much the same processes as Earth does," Arren said. "We should have some dinner anyway, aren't you guys starving? You haven't eaten since we left home."

That's when Chase realised he was famished.

"You... have a garden?"

"Sure, help me up."

They hobbled down a few corridors, each looking like they'd been made by an entirely different interior designer who'd never even met the last one. They passed through a random collection of doors: sleek self-opening exits that sung when opened, huge metallic portals that had to be opened by a noisy hand winch, and through strange curtains of blue material that clung to them as they walked by.

Eventually they arrived at the garden. It was gigantic, the size of a big park on Earth. There was enough room for the birds inside to fly around, and all sorts of living creatures skittering along the ground. It was nice, really nice, and an artificial sun kept everything warm.

"This place keeps me sane," said Arren. "Though the Coebri used to mess it all up all the time. They're polluters, you know. Only out to make money, then spend it on their own pleasures, never thinking about long term plans. I hate them."

"Well, you can forget about them now, remember?" Chase said.

"Yes, yes I can," Arren agreed, and sitting on some stones by a tinkling brook watched them set up the picnic lunch their dad had prepared.

She wasn't impressed with the neatly cut peanut butter and jam sandwiches or even the lettuce and cheese sandwich. She pulled the lettuce out and ate it, while they downed everything else in moments.

After a minute, she seemed hungry again and hobbled to a nearby tree to pick some fruit for them. It tasted to Chase like a mix between apples and blackberries, and it was delicious.

Then she dug her hands into the dirt under some bushes and pulled out some roots that looked like large green carrots. She washed them in the stream and started to eat them raw.

"Mmm, Modleuom," she gloated, "Try these, lots of fibre!"

They did try one each. Chase thought they were pretty nice, but a bit bland, like raw potatoes; you wouldn't want to live on them.

"What I can't understand," Arren said, "is why you people don't *live* on these? They're delicious! And why do you have to *fry* everything? You eat so much meat! It takes ten times more land to feed a person living on mostly meat than a person living on mostly vegetables."

"Really?" Chase asked.

"Well, according to Wikipedia[22]." Arren smiled.

She still wasn't going to tell them something they weren't supposed to know.

"So, where to now?" Chase asked after the meal was finished.

"I don't know," she answered.

"What do you think Chase?" Lucky asked.

"I asked the question first," he argued.

"Didn't you hear?" Lucky said. "You're in charge now. We even took one from the silver man just to make sure."

"What?!" Chase gawked in disbelief.

"It's true," Arren said. "Back in the control room, you claimed this ship as your own. That includes me. So until the Unity arrives and tries to force me back to the Coebri, you're in charge. Or unless the Coebri arrive and claim me back, then we've got a fight on our hands."

"In charge... really?" Chase said.

"Really!" Arren smiled. "Well, more or less."

---

[22] Look up "Environmental vegetarianism" for some really interesting arguments for why everyone should try eating more vegetables!

"Lucky dude, you just got yourself a spaceship!" Lucky teased.

Chase's head was spinning. How did *this* happen?

"Then I…" He began.

She put her hand on his, again. "That's how we were able to get away. You gave me permission to get away and I did. Otherwise, I would've had to obey the tracker and take you back to Earth. So for now, you're the legal owner of this ship."

Chase just sat there, scratching his head, still a little bemused by the whole situation.

"I don't know. I don't know where we should go. Arren, where do you think?"

She smiled. "Cambriania. I've read about it my *whole life*. It's not part of the Unity, and it's not Coebri, so we should be able to hide there for quite some time. At least until we're sure I'm safe."

"Sounds good to me."

"We shouldn't leave just yet, the repairs aren't finished."

"Yeah, about that," Lucky said. "What I don't get is what happened while we were cutting out the arm before. Why'd we lose track of everyone? That was pretty freaky."

"I fainted," Arren said. "But the automatic defence mechanisms took over. The ship and I are almost finished repairing, we should be able to travel anywhere we want to in about eight hours."

"That's great, but does that explain what happened to my gravity boots? And the head set?" Chase asked.

"What?" She said, sounding confused.

"The boots stopped working. And the headset," he explained.

It looked like Arren did not believe him.

"Are you sure, I mean, it wasn't just you was it?" She asked.

He smiled. She really didn't seem to think much of Earthlings. "No, I really don't think so."

"Hmm," she said, and looked straight ahead as if she was looking at a screen that only she could see.

"The boots are damaged… the headset, its power is drained…" She said, still puzzled. "You sure nothing else happened out there?"

"Well… I think I saw a green flash of light, but what's that–"

"Oh no, that'd explain it!" She said, getting angry and standing up. Suddenly lightning flashed all around the roof.

"Get off!" She screamed, and throwing her arms out in front of her let out another mighty yell. The ship lurched once again but not as violently as when the tracker was stuck on.

She sat down, exhausted.

"That's enough of that for one day, eh!" Chase said.

She brushed down her clothes. "Yes boss," and smiled.

"Care to explain?" Lucky said.

"Look!" She replied.

The roof was opening up, the metal sliding back as the light came in. Bright, brilliant red light. Soon the ceiling opened to reveal an enormous supergiant sun.

"Hello, Aldebaran[23]," she said, and warmed her hands in its glow. "Just a little wormhole, not too far this time. They were spies, more Will-o's. So very dangerous," she said,

---

[23] <u>Aldebaran</u> is a star visible from earth, a red supergiant star about 44 times bigger than our sun. From earth, it is the brightest star in the constellation of Taurus, and one of the brightest stars in the night sky. Yet at the speed of light it would still take 65 million years to get there!

almost asleep. "They must have broken the suit, trying to get us back to the Coebri. They're gone now."

"Ahh, Arren?" Chase said.

"Sorry. I gotta sleep. You find your beds, Lopi will take you. Beds, Lopi? Yes. I like the gard..." and she was asleep.

Chase didn't like leaving her there, but the boa constrictor was pretty persuasive. He figured that if she wanted to take a nap in the middle of her garden she probably knew what she was doing. It was nice, even the plants seemed to bend down to cover her from the bright red light as they left.

"What do you make of all this?" Lucky asked as they followed the snake.

"... Pretty exciting," Chase said.

Lucky smiled. "Yes, and all that. Now... what do you *really* think of all this?"

Chase hated his brother sometimes. He could not remember a time, ever, EVER, that he'd managed to keep a secret from him.

Then again, maybe this wasn't the time to keep secrets.

"I'm a bit scared. This is all pretty crazy. I think Arren might be in more trouble than we can handle."

"Hmmm."

"And I can't believe the stupid Universal Unity won't help her! How can they leave her like this? What are they, some kind of monsters? She's a *slave*. No one should be a slave."

"Hmmm."

"Not too sure I like my first look of the universe beyond our little blue planet," Chase confessed. "How about you?"

"Hmmm," Lucky mumbled, not saying a thing.

Lucky's silence angered Chase, but he was too tired to argue; then he realised he could not remember a time, ever, EVER, that Lucky couldn't keep a secret from *him*.

Jerk.

Lopi led the way to a large room with twenty beds. The Coebri seemed to have slept on hard stones topped with only a thin rubber sheet, but they collapsed on the beds anyway and fell asleep in minutes.

And as he did, Chase's last thought was: *gee, I hope Dad's all right... and Arren too...*

***

Next morning, or the time Chase decided was morning, he tiptoed back towards the garden. Arren was up already, seemingly back to normal. She was making herself busy, fixing an egg and eggplant breakfast with some strange milk from the little, soft-toed goats that wandered around her indoor garden. It smelt delicious.

He walked up to her cooking on some kind of small floating BBQ among the trees and river.

"Good morning Chase," she said.

"Morning."

"Sleep well?" She asked, looking for his answer.

"Yup, thank you," he said.

She looked at him for a moment.

"Really?" She asked.

He sighed. Someone *else* he couldn't keep secrets from.

"Not really, I kept having nightmares. Those green lights really freaked me out," he admitted.

She sighed.

"I thought they might," she said, fiddling with breakfast. "You have powerful fear; it's how they latch on. They'll find their way back if we don't do something about it... Can I offer you something?" She asked.

"Sure," he agreed.

"I could give you a scientifically advanced device to wear, even disguise it as a watch or necklace, but you'd just end up losing it or giving it away to the wrong person one day. Besides, why risk it when we can do a little rearranging? Just a few tweaks of the DNA[24], subtle altering of your human energy field[25]. Nothing serious, just… putting you in a better state of balance," she offered.

"What do you mean?" He asked.

"Have you ever heard the saying that you only use ten per cent of your brain?" She asked.

"Yes," he replied, a little unsure of what she was getting at, or if he was willing to participate in an alien experiment, especially one involving his brain.

"Well, it's completely untrue! Just about all humans use almost one hundred per cent of their brain, and those that don't are either in a coma or seriously disadvantaged. It's a misquote and a rumour to say you only use ten per cent of your brain[26]! It's more accurate to say you and your brother are only using ten per cent of your brain and body's *potential*. Imagine if you could roll a maths genius, sports genius, and musical genius all into one person, not three? It is possible, once you start using all your body's potential. In a way it's what your people are trying to do, change, improve, grow. You're living longer, learning faster, you're finding ways to unlock humanity's potential. I'd just speed

---

[24] Stands for Deoxyribonucleic acid. It's considered the 'code of life' – the chemical inside our cells that's responsible for keeping them, and us, alive and running.

[25] The human energy field is the name given to the electromagnetic field around people, some believing it may be the human aura. Again, science has yet to conclusively support the idea of the human aura, but some people claim they can see it.

[26] Check out "10percent" on www.snopes.com

up that process for you, only in one or two areas. It doesn't take much, just a little balancing of your natural potential. Potential that's already there."

"So I wouldn't change, become some freak?"

"I don't know how you'd define freak, but no. You'd just be a better you."

"Ok," he agreed, still a little reluctant.

"Good," she said. "Because it won't work without your permission."

She held out her hand and a silver ball of light gathered in her palm. She held it up and it floated over to rest on the top of his head. Slowly, the silver light gently flowed down, surrounding his skin and dissolving into his body.

He didn't feel a thing. No laser vision, no super hearing. Just a few random thoughts, then he felt a little calmer.

"Now what?" He asked.

"It'll probably take a while, but at least those alien attachments won't be a problem anymore. May I ask what were you thinking about?" She questioned.

"I was, well, this is going to sound silly. But the day we met you, we were running away from a bully, that Mark T kid you know from school. I lost to him in a rocket contest. He took my five dollars, smashed up my launcher and was going to beat me up too! I... I was so angry about that, I *really* wanted to get back at him. But now I think I just feel sorry for him, it's like he only knows how to be a bully. I wonder what life is like for him at home? What makes a guy so mean like that? Really, it was just a stupid rocket contest."

"Seeing things from a new perspective?" She asked.

"Yeah, I mean, I'd still like to win but it's not about making him look stupid any more. It's just weird. Do you get what I mean?"

She smiled. "Sure, I think that's pretty mature of you, actually."

"Did you do that?" He asked, referring to the silver light, since there was no known technology on Earth that could do what she just did.

"Not really. Just, bringing out what was already there."

"Can you do it again?" He asked, wondering if it might help Lucky get a better grip on schooling.

"No, not like that. It's just... not like that," she said cryptically. "Kind of... being a part of this ship I can... do certain things. But I can't do other things. Not like a normal human. The way I was made, I only get to do that once," she said.

Before Chase could ponder further Lucky turned up, yawning wider than a sleepy tiger.

"Sup," he said, half asleep. But then he smelt breakfast and woke right up. "Ooh, food!"

Chase laughed.

"Breakfast for three!" Arren said. "Beats having to feed a hundred. Gee, the Coebri were slobs, I never realised!"

After they'd eaten a healthy breakfast they all moved up to the control room.

"So, off to Cambriania?" Arren asked.

"Yes, take us to Cambriania!" Chase ordered confidently.

Arren giggled. "Certainly, but first, you should know. They are a powerful, proud people. Two points of difference between their culture and yours. First, staring is considered very rude. Actually, it is in most of the places in the Unity. You're going to want to stare a lot, so don't. Second, don't touch any girls. It's *really* against the rules there. And I mean *really*. Now, you're both off-worlders so they're likely to give you some leeway but they appreciate the effort, so try OK? Just let me do the talking."

"Why, you afraid we might say something and get us thrown into jail?" Lucky teased.

"No, you don't speak the language," Arren replied, never sure when he was kidding or not. Then she smiled. "I think you'll like Cambriania."

The stars suddenly rushed towards them, just like in the movies.

"Nothing like faster-than-light travel when you get the chance." Arren smiled.

Chapter 6
Cambriania

It took about twenty minutes to get there. Arren informed them that Cambriania was about four thirds the volume of Earth, but not as dense, so they would only feel a little bit heavier. The surface was eighty per cent jungle, surrounding numerous giant lakes. At the poles the jungle thinned out to become arboreal pine forests, which was as cold as it got on Cambriania. It sounded interesting.

She negotiated a landing deal right away, but it took a little over an hour to safely and gently enter the atmosphere.

"Why's it taking so long?" Lucky whinged.

"The people of Cambriania have a very traditional approach to planetary entry. It takes this long to drop from orbit, using the atmosphere to help slow us down," she said.

"What, like the old space shuttle?" Chase asked.

"Yes, just like that," she said.

"I don't get it," Lucky asked. "How's air supposed to slow you down?"

She looked over at him and furrowed her brow. "Ever opened the car window while it's driving along?" She asked.

"Well, duh," he replied.

"Well," she explained. "What happens to your hand?"

"It gets pushed around by the wind," he said.

"That's right. Even if there's no breeze outside, if the car is moving there'll be air moving against the car. Now, imagine what would happen if the car wasn't moving at, like, a hundred kilometres an hour on the freeway back on Earth. Imagine it's falling towards the planet at fifteen *kilometres per second.* Even bullets don't go fifteen kilometres *per second*. What's that going to do to your hand?" She asked.

He looked thoughtful. "It'd get ripped right off, I reckon," he said.

"It would, and all that air squished up in front heats up our spaceship. Air isn't nothing, it's something – like water only much thinner. But it still takes up space, and weighs something, and you have to push all that something out of the way if you want to move through it. And if you want to move very quickly, it can sometimes be *a lot* of air to move out of the way. Tonnes in fact. Tonnes and tonnes of air being pushed out of the way every second that we fly this little spaceship towards the surface of a planet. *That's a lot.* That's why most asteroids burn up before they even hit the ground, they crash into the air super-fast and it heats them up to burning point. Atmospheric entry is fairly simple but you still need to be careful about it," Arren explained[27].

Lucky looked thoughtful.

"Wow," said Chase.

Then Arren handed them some plain brown robes to wear over their normal clothes while she put on an emerald green one, like a kimono.

"This is the fashion at this time of year." She smiled.

"Yeah, I bet it's what they're *all* wearing." Lucky moaned.

After landing, they each took another sonic shower and sunbath. Then, for the first time ever, Chase and Lucky stood on the ground of another world.

---

[27] Asteroids enter so quickly and they heat up so much that they can burn. However, they're also so fast that, if they're large enough and have a side that does not press against the air, it does not heat up much at all. Asteroids can arrive melted on one side and frozen on the other!

"Oh. Seems she's right about the outfits," Lucky observed. It really was what everyone was wearing, though Arren's bright green outfit stood out a bit.

Cambriania was beautiful! The air was fresh and humid, the sun bright and yellow. The buildings were amazing, not like anything on Earth. They curved upwards in giant skyscrapers yet there was so much jungle between them they just looked like enormous blades of grass from far way.

Everything seemed to be made with great care, made to endure. Even the ground around the landing platform was polished granite stones, well cared for, with rich bronze and gold inlays.

The people looked a lot like people from Earth, most were a gentle shade of brown. It wasn't hard to tell the difference between guys and girls. The guys wore almost all brown robes and walked in ones or twos. The girls were in much larger and much more colourful groups, and never sat near the men. Indeed, it seemed that when a flying bus came along it was for either guys or girls. Everyone else looked like they walked wherever they went as there didn't seem to be any cars.

"Wow, is everything on this planet so nice?" Chase asked.

"Yes, this is what can happen when the wealth on a world is shared equally," Arren explained.

That's when he noticed there was a group of about a dozen people waiting to greet them.

Arren walked up, clapped her hands and did a little bow towards them. The women came up, talked to her and put wreaths of white flowers around her neck. At the same time, three men approached Chase and Lucky. They were holding a handful of smoking leaves and began blowing and pushing the smoke all over them.

"What's this for?" Chase asked.

"Smudging," Arren explained, putting one hand on top of each of the women's outstretched hands, one at a time, in an odd kind of greeting.

Lucky coughed and waved away the smoke.

"You're off-worlders," she smiled. "They are cleaning you and chasing away evil spirits. Very common tradition for newcomers."

"Really?' Chase said, not sure whether she meant evil spirits literally or not.

"Weird," Lucky said.

"Yeah, right," Arren said with a cheeky smile, "like no one ever smudges you on Earth, oh, except the Australian Aborigines[28], and the American Indians, and etcetera, etcetera, etcetera!"

"Owned," Chase teased him.

"Still weird," Lucky blinked and waved away the smoke.

The Cambrianian men smiled and stood back.

Then Arren turned while one of them spoke. She translated: "Earthling men, Chase and Lucky, all who come in peace are welcome. All who come with love in their hearts are family. We invite you to share in the bounty of our table."

"Really?" Lucky said enthusiastically.

"Hey, it's Cambriania," she replied.

The men spoke to Arren again, indicating towards the ship. Then she translated: "Earthling Chase, I ask your permission to tend to your ship and its needs while you rest. Is this well with you? I mean, is this alright with you?"

Chase looked at Arren, she nodded.

"Sure," he said.

---

[28] Try a web search, for example Yahoo Answers, and search for "what is an aboriginal smoking ceremony" for more details.

The man seemed to find that funny, perhaps it was something about the word 'sure', but then he placed his hand on Chase's chest, closed his eyes and muttered a prayer or blessing.

Arren didn't translate, but smiled. "Welcome to Cambriania."

They had a communal lunch of exotic fruits and vegetables, with a fish dish that Chase didn't recognise. Everyone was very friendly and helpful. But the men and woman sat separately, which meant Lucky and Chase had no idea what was going on because Arren was too far away to translate for them. Still, the Cambrianians seemed to be quite patient and tolerant of those that did not speak their language.

After the lunch they were guests of honour at a dance; guests from Earth, Arren told them, were understandably quite rare. The women went up to put floral wreaths around their necks and Lucky was going to help them till Chase held his hands down. They really appreciated that.

After the dance was the obligatory massage. At least Arren said it was obligatory. Yet the gender rules still applied so Chase and Lucky were massaged by a pair of Cambrianian men who resembled Titans. They looked like they should be on some kind of muscle man contest but apparently enjoyed giving deep tissue massages even more. Their forearms were *huge*.

It was very relaxing but after an hour or so Chase was beginning to feel a little concerned about getting free food and massages instead of being at school, so he decided to locate Arren. After all, he realised, they had no idea how long they were actually going to be there, or where they would stay – though he felt that it wouldn't be a problem. Everyone here was only too happy to help. After a while he and Lucky managed to locate Arren chatting gaily with a dozen other girls her age. They looked quite interested in what she had to say but stopped talking and almost squealed when they saw boys approaching.

Arren finished what she was saying, dismissed the group, and turned towards them.

"That was a class of students. They wanted to speak to me. So, what do you think of Cambriania? Nice, hey? Could stay here for a while?" She said, sounding hopeful.

"Yeah, why is everyone so *nice*?" Lucky asked.

"They weren't always," she replied. "They've had wars, much like Earth. But they overcame their major problems ten thousand years or so ago, now they live in peace. It can be done you know, it really can."

"They are very friendly," Chase said.

"Yes, it's a policy here, based on a highly advanced scientific understanding of social processes, including reciprocal kindness, inter-species reputation management and fun."

"Fun?" Chase said, wondering what the science was in 'fun'[29].

"Yes, they believe it's fun to be nice."

"Whatever, but hey, what's with the outfits?" Lucky interrupted.

"That's just Lobromia, the nation we're on, deeply religious. Kzentia is much more secular and clothes a little more varied, but Lobromia *defines* Cambriania."

"Oh, so there are different nations here, too," Lucky realised out loud.

---

[29] There's loads of science in fun! You can start with the "Oxford handbook of positive psychology." By C. R. Snyder & Shane J. Lopez.

"Of course!" She said again, as if she was wondering why on earth he'd never thought of that before. "What, do you think each planet only has *one* culture to offer?"

Lucky shrugged.

"Anyway," Chase interrupted. "How long do you think they'll let us stay?"

"As long as we like, though a welcome will usually wear out in about two months if you don't start contributing. We can start today, they're always looking for pickers for the fruit harvests, or you might try teaching them English, they'd just love that!"

"Wait, you're going to put us to work?" Chase said, "What about school? We haven't even finished high school!"

"Chase!" Lucky said. "You're on an alien planet wondering about how you'll pass school? Forget school!"

"No, you're right," Arren said. "You... oh, I'd forgotten about that. You'll have to take out citizenships, that way it won't pollute your race's unconscious mind."

"Really?" Chase said.

"Really, and then they'd expect you to takes wives..." She said.

"What?!" Chase choked. He'd never even thought about marriage, didn't think he'd have to think about it for a few years yet!

"Of course, you don't get passed age two on Cambriania without the promise of an arranged wife," Arren explained in a matter-of-fact way.

"Umm, I'm think I'm not liking this idea so much right now," Chase worried.

"Why not? Marriage is quite common on your world, even in Australia," she said, looking puzzled.

"Oh, I think *I* can make the sacrifice," Lucky joked.

"What?" Chase panicked, "No Lucky, we are not getting married, yet. But how long do we have to stay? Aren't you worried that the Coebri might find us here?" He was trying to be a bit more real about the situation.

"Eventually, yes, but they're very unpopular here. We should stay … a night at least. I'm trading several of my old Coebri items for fuel and equipment."

"I got the impression they didn't use money."

"They don't, but they have very strong moral beliefs about not taking more than they give. They do trade, but their version of value can be very interesting. They take gold about as seriously as bronze, for instance. There's not much copper on Cambriania, one reason why the Coebri try and sneak in to trade…"

"Arren, you're a wealth of information," Lucky interrupted, "but I think we might like to look into those citizenships a bit more. I *really* like it here!"

Chase was beginning to get annoyed at his brother's silly requests but before he could think any more, the old man who'd given him a blessing suddenly appeared on the steps near where they were talking. Literally. It wasn't like he walked in or anything, just one moment he wasn't there, and the next he was, staring at them intently, like something was wrong.

"Earth-man Chase," he said right to him with a mild accent. "They are coming."

Arren gasped.

She spoke to him quickly in his language and in reply he pushed his bottom lip out in a gesture that might have meant yes.

"Come!" She ordered them and started walking away at her incredible pace.

"What is it?" Chase said. "I didn't know he could speak English."

"He doesn't, it's a gift," she said, looking over at Chase. "You Earthlings have so much to relearn. But you heard him, *they're coming.*"

"Who?" Lucky said, hurrying to catch up.

"The Universal Unity," she replied.

"When?" Chase said, starting to feel worried.

"I hope... no! Get away from the ship!" She yelled at the top of her lungs. But there was no way anyone who was near the ship could hear her. They were still a kilometre or two away from the landing platform.

"Move, move!" She ordered, and started running out of the courtyard and right down the main street.

"Bit sooner than you'd hoped, hey?" Lucky teased and sighed. "I liked Cambriania..."

"No. They're too fast!" Arren shouted.

They were in trouble again.

"Move, move!" She repeated, then suddenly stopped running and turned her back to them. "Boys, back up against me!"

She pressed up against them, back to back.

Citizens were scandalised, especially a posse of young girls, at the unsightly scene of three youths of *different genders* standing back to back. A mother covered her child's eyes, and someone dropped a pile of sticks on the ground and fainted clear away.

"What, what's happening?" Lucky asked, looking around.

Suddenly Chase saw, rapidly approaching from up the street, narrowly skimming between the sharp skyscrapers of Cambriania, the ship. His ship. He watched as most of it began to disappear into whatever dimension it usually stayed in, leaving only the tiny UFO section with the door.

The wide open door.

"Stay close, don't move!" Arren ordered. Then with prodigious precision she slammed the entire ship down on top of them.

That was when Chase discovered that going from a standing up position into a diverse gravity field was a rather violent way of getting into a spaceship. The three of them were thrown face first onto the floor of the entrance. Automatically the shower turned on before the outer door had even finished closing.

"No, no, no!" Arren shouted, scrambling to her feet. "Up!" she ordered the ship and began hauling open the inner doors.

Immediately, she was thrown backwards by a hurricane of air, only grabbing on to the door at the last second to prevent being thrown out into the vacuum of space. The outer door was stuck half-closed. They'd gone into space before they'd been able to close it. Lucky and Chase were thrown to the floor.

"Close the door!" Lucky shouted, scrambling desperately across the floor to prevent being thrown out too. "We'll be sucked into space!"

"Not sucked, pushed!" Arren corrected. "It's the air pressure inside the ship that is pushing us out into space."

"So, close the inside door," Lucky shouted.

"She can't!" Chase realised. "The air in here will all rush out and we'll suffocate."

"Then explode," Arren finished for him.

"So, do *something*!"

Chase looked back at the outside door, only barely noticing how surprisingly calm he felt. He saw that the outside hatch was still ajar, then realised why: all the air rushing against it was keeping it open. If he could stop the air there, even for a second, it might be enough to get the outside hatch closed.

He thought about using his own body like a plug but then realised that if he did the amount of air pushing against him would still be enough to break his back and push him out into space anyway. Air had pressure – air was pushing all the time and it was pushing very hard. [30]

Arren cried out. She was losing her grip.

Chase slid sideways along the floor until he came to a panel. Heaving against it, he tried to pry it free. Arren saw what he was doing and stared at the panel hard. Suddenly, there was a shower of golden sparks and the panel fell off.

It wasn't as large as the door, but it might do. Chase tried to angle the panel as the wind attempted to rip it out of his hands.

"Chase!" Lucky screamed as he started slipping towards the exit.

Trusting that Lucky was still lucky, Chase let go of the panel.

It flew out of his hands and wacked against the exit. The hurricane suddenly decreased. Then two of the spider robots hauled the door shut from the outside. As they slammed it shut, the wind suddenly died.

"That was close," Lucky said, standing up and trembling a little.

"Too close," Arren said, looking shaken. She ran towards the control room, Lucky and Chase close behind. When they got there, the screens were a riot of colour and motion. It looked like they were whizzing through entirely different

---

[30] Remember: Wind is not the same as air pressure! Wind happens in only one direction and only sometimes. Air pressure is all around you, all the time.

regions of space every second. First, they were near a giant asteroid belt. Then they were racing past a blue sun.

"Did we lose them?" Lucky asked.

"Lose them?" Arren shouted, looking indignant.

"Just wondering," he muttered in apology.

She spoke softly, "It's a Nova Class, high-end, multidimensional, Universal Unity star craft. No, we have *not* lost them!"

"Do we fight?" Lucky asked, glancing at his fence paling still sitting on the deck where he'd left it.

Arren didn't answer.

"Well! Don't you have some kinds of weapons on this thing?" He nearly shouted.

"I'd *never* use the weapons to harm others," she said in absolute determination.

Suddenly, their ship jolted sideways.

A voice sounded inside their minds.

Mining vessel, you have trespassed Earth space and are carrying two unlicensed Earthlings with you. Stop at once.

"No," Chase shouted, "Arren, get us out of here!"

Then a massive, glowing, yellow net appeared all around them.

Arren grunted and the ship images shimmered. They hit the net head on. Slowly, somehow, they kept on going. Arren squealed and a second later they were out.

"Phew, that was close," Arren said. The locations on the screens shifted several more times then there was silence.

One minute.

Then two.

"I think we lost them," Lucky finally risked speaking.

Three minutes.

Arren sat back in relief. "That was *too close*," she said.

Chapter 7
Rlaeiul

Four minutes.

"So," Chase finally broke the silence, "Where to now?"

Arren was quiet for several breaths. "I guess the Unity is on our tail, so I'm not sure where we should go."

"Here's a suggestion," Lucky offered, "Why don't we try one of the Unity worlds? You know, hide right under their noses?"

Arren blinked at him, like she couldn't make sense of what he'd just said. "I'd... never have thought of that," she finally replied.

Then she brightened. "Yes! That's a great idea! And I know just where to go! One of the places that's reasonably new to the Unity. Gentlemen, prepare for your first tour of Rlaeiul!"

"Ray oo..." Lucky tried to pronounce.

"No, no, the first sound is halfway between an R and an L, just like in Japanese. The rest of the sounds are vowels or soft consonants. RL - ay - ee - oo - l," she pronounced, the oo sounding very much like a deep U, like in French.

"R... L... Rayeeool," Chase settled on, doing the best he could.

She laughed.

"Rlaeiul," she pronounced. Then the screens changed again.

A moment later they were staring at a blue-green gas giant, like Neptune, only it must have been as large as Jupiter. There was a white sun, very far away. Circling the blue gas giant was a little, white-blue planet, not much bigger than Mars.

"Rlaeiul," Arren explained, pointing to the little planet, "Population two billionish, very peaceful. But what makes this planet really special is that the life forms on it don't get their energy from the sun. Their entire food chain is based on the plants being able to get their energy from the massive magnetic field between Rlaeiul and its blue gas giant planet. No photosynthesis at all..."

"Really?" Chase asked in disbelief.

"Yep. Just like the extremophiles back on Earth who use chemosynthesis, not photosynthesis to get their energy.[31] Scratch yet another expected necessary quality of life!" She said.

"How do they collect magnetism?" Chase wondered.

"They use little iron rich spirals inside their cells to gather energy. As long as the magnetic field is always moving they have life, day in and day out. Magnetic creatures able to sense magnetic fields.[32] You'll like them I think. But remember, culturally Rlaeiul is, well, it's different. It's not like any other world you've been on."

"How's it different?" Lucky wanted to know.

"For one thing, no lying. No stealing. Very big rules here." She turned around, getting serious. "Very big rules. On worlds, such as this one and the others who are part of the Universal Unity, lying is about as bad as bad people get. It can get you thrown into jail for life. It's about as bad... as murder is on your world."

"I can see why you have such a problem with us Earthlings," Lucky said.

---

[30] Search "Extrophiles" online. (See my website for active links).

[32] I made these up, no known magnetosynthesists exist in nature.

"Even the Coebri keep their oaths better than Earthlings," Arren lectured. "You guys are a novelty, but don't go upsetting people. It could be very, very bad for you."

"What about you?" Lucky said. "Didn't you break a rule or something?"

She gave him an angry look and stalked off.

"Don't upset her," Chase told him.

"Why not?" Lucky asked. He probably thought upsetting people was part of the job description of what it meant to be Lucky.

***

An hour later the Rlaeiul government gave permission to land and they slipped through the atmosphere in seconds without touching it, just like they did once back on Earth. Two minutes later they were on the surface getting ready to disembark.

"Now," she explained, "I don't really have time to acclimatise you to the difference in air pressure here, like I did on Cambriania. There you didn't even notice, did you? Well, here the air is so thin that it's like living on the top of Mount Everest. Hikers can take up to two weeks to adapt to the low pressure and oxygen levels. So I think it's best if we wear the suits again," she announced, "at least most of the time."

"What if I need to take a pee?" Lucky asked.

"Just wait till you get back on the ship to pee, Lucky!" She stated, glaring at him.

"Awww," he pretended to complain.

"It's like this," she said, deciding he needed a deeper explanation about the dangers of removing space suits.

"Picture the air is made out of billions of little particles, like oxygen and nitrogen. And those particles aren't just floating around, they're whizzing around like high speed tennis balls, always bouncing and never slowing down unless they get colder, right? You can imagine that? All that bouncing creates what we call *air pressure*. Air is always pushing in all directions all the time. Even though the individual particles are very small, so small you can knock them out of the way with your hand, altogether they're incredibly strong."

"Go on, how strong?" He asked, slipping into his helmet.

"On a space the size of your fingernail, about a kilogram."

"So?"

"So, over your whole body that's more than a tonne," she said, just a little exasperated. "You've more than a car's worth of weight in *air* pressing in on you right now!"

"That's unbelievable."

"Well believe it," she instructed. "Still, the air's pretty thin here, there are less bouncing particles of air than you are used to. It's still breathable, but you're only Earthlings, so I'm not going to risk it."

"So what else can air pressure do?" Chase asked. Arren seemed to like explaining things, besides, he was curious.

"Heaps," Arren replied. "Regions of high and low pressure help create the weather on Earth: the wind blows from a region of high pressure to low pressure. Also, you can't drink from a straw without the outside air helping to push down on your drink so that it'll flow into your mouth. Did you know that? You can't 'suck' air in, you only make a gap in your mouth and the outside air pushes the drink in. Isn't that amazing! Oh, and most explosions are just really large amounts of very hot air being created suddenly– from the little explosions in your car that make it go, to atomic bomb blasts[33]. Air pressure is being put to work all the time and you didn't even know!"

"Who'd have thought a billion little bouncing balls could make such a difference?" Lucky mused.

Perhaps he could be taught science, Chase thought, *if his life was threatened by suffocation on an alien world.* Still, Chase thought it was pretty amazing too. A billion little balls bouncing in every direction, all the time, with enough pressure to lift you off your feet[34].

The air hissed out of the airlock and their suits clamped down on them. Then they stepped out.

Rlaeiul was blue. There were yellows and browns, but mostly, it was blue. The sky was a light blue like the horizon on Earth, and the grass, the trees, even the people were every shade of indigo, navy, or just plain blue. They'd landed in what looked like a field or park, but there were a few other spaceships unloading people and cargo.

In the low gravity everything had a chance to grow taller, so the people of Rlaeiul were huge – some were almost three meters tall. It made Chase feel very small and unusual. The people wore blue shorts and shirts, and little beaded necklaces. They looked like lanky humans with white hair, but they were so very blue.

---

[33] Guns use hot air too: a mini explosion caused by chemicals catching on fire inside the gun to push the bullet out. That explosion also pushes the gun in the opposite direction, causing the 'kickback' you feel.

[33] Seriously! <u>Draw your foot</u> on a piece of 1cm grid paper. For each square centimeter there is, roughly, 1 kilogram of air pressure pushing on it. With two feet the average middle school student might have about 70 kilograms of pressure under their feet! Do you weigh less than 70 kilograms? Yes? Then the air pressure under your feet could lift you right off the ground and smash you into the roof – if there was no air above you to help keep you down!

"Does the magnetism make them blue?" Chase asked.

"There's a lot of silver in the diet, necessary for the plants to metabolise magnetic energy. A condition I believe your people call Argyria? Here there's nothing healthier than a rich blue tint to your skin!" Arren explained.

They looked out at the blue people walking around and, for the most part, ignoring them.

"What, no welcoming committee?" Lucky sighed.

"No, they expect you to just intuit your way around here," she said.

"Intuit?" Chase asked.

"Yes, very intuitive people. They probably knew we were coming as soon as we made the decision, probably as soon as we asked the question. They'll have a welcome planned; we just need to intuit where it will be."

"That's odd," Chase said.

Arren pushed him to the front. "Intuition's your department Chase."

"Me? But... wh... do they do *everything* by intuition?" He asked.

"Not everyone thinks like your people do," she said. "Exploring the universe is as much an adventure in culture as it is in science."

He looked around.

Intuition. Hmmm. Am I just supposed to feel welcome? Probably a good way to sort out the insincere from sincere visitors. Everyone looked pretty relaxed among the trees and grasses of this nature loving place, there were no roads even in this transport hub. As he looked further out he could see that all the buildings were short and round, made of stone or dirt, except they all seemed to have large upward standing loops and spirals. *Perhaps to catch the magnetic field?*

"You know," Lucky asked Arren, "on Earth they're always checking passports and that sort of stuff. How come none of that happens out here?"

"I took care of that before we arrived," she answered.

"I just had an idea," Chase said, "Is there some kind of restaurant or hotel where we can take these suits off? I don't think I can stay like this all day."

"Yeah, maybe see what they have on TV! I wonder what passes for humour among this lot," Lucky said enthusiastically.

"Well... there's the Auroran Lookout. It's a big hotel here. They say it's good for food, and it's got pressurised apartments," Arren said. "Besides, they have toilets so it's good news for you, hey Lucky!"

"Ha, ha," he said with a sarcastic grin. "Well, how do we get there, Chase?"

Chase didn't hear the answer. His eyes had caught a little Rlaeiulian boy. Little, because even though he was at least a head taller than Chase, he looked a year or so younger. He had dark blue shorts, dark indigo coloured eyes and short white hair much like everyone else. Chase couldn't help looking over at him, as though the boy was waiting for Chase to talk to him or something.

So, with the other two looking on, he walked through the wavy blue grass and said hello.

The boy stared at him, then smiled.

"It's just a kid," Arren explained to Chase.

"A stranger to our world?" The blue boy asked in flawless English. "Little pink boy with a bowl on his head. Where are you from?"

Arren's mouth dropped open in surprise, but Chase just answered, "We're from Earth and we're looking around. What's your name?" He asked.

The boy answered, but his pronunciation was strange. It started with something like 'Moiya'.

Lucky joined them. "Well, then we'll call you Moiya."

The boy smiled. At least *that* was recognisable.

"I guess we found our guide," Arren said.

"Moiya," Chase asked, ignoring the fact that Lucky was renaming people again. "Can you help us? We're looking to go to the Auroran Lookout."

The young boy's eyes widened in excitement. "Auroran Lookout! That is the most special place on Rlaeiul. Yes, yes, I can take you." He said, and putting his hand to his mouth, gave four piercing whistles.

"What about your parents?" Chase wondered.

The boy looked confused. "They are at home," he stated.

"They'll know where he is and if he's about to get into any trouble," Arren assured him.

"Wow. Kinda trusting around here, aren't they?" Lucky muttered.

"Yeah. As I said, they do everything by intuition," she tried to explain.

Then, emerging from the grasslands at a terrific speed, were four of the strangest creatures Chase had ever seen. They looked like giant blue-grey kangaroos, except they ran instead of hopped. Their backbones were strangely transparent too, so that he could see rings of red tissue attached to their spines, probably for catching, or detecting, the planet's magnetism.

"No faster way to travel than by wobegot." Moiya smiled. He helped the visitors to make friends with the strange, agitated beasts.

The wobegot had no saddles, so Chase found he had to stand on its hips and hold on really tight to its neck.

"I've heard about these..." Arren said, grinning broadly but looking nervous. "Better hold on tight!"

As soon as they were ready, Moiya leapt on his beast and off they went. The four wobegots tore through the grass at breakneck speed and kept getting faster. Then suddenly, they all jumped.

But it wasn't a normal jump, not visibly from one place to another. Everything went blurry for a second as if they were travelling through space itself. They did it again and again, hopping through space. The blue gas giant kept moving across the sky in jerky leaps. After only a few minutes they were far away from where their ship had landed, perhaps on the other side of the planet.

Moiya dismounted and waved off their mounts.

"Won't we need them for later?" Lucky asked.

Moiya smiled. "They will be here when we need them, not sooner. But this will only work if we trust them and let them go now." He smiled, and bending over kissed the ground in what might have been a gesture of gratitude.

It was a *very* different place.

"Look!" Moiya said, and pointed towards the sky.

There, above them in the sky, the most incredible lightshow of colour and motion Chase had ever seen was just beginning. It was just like the Aurora Australis[35] at home, only a hundred times brighter and vastly more colourful. Even the ground kept changing colour in the reflected light.

"The Southern Auroras are the brightest," Arren explained in awe, her voiced muffled in reverence. "But I'd never imagined them to be like this! Rlaeiul has a magnetic field hundreds of times stronger than Earth's field and

---

[34] Aurora Borealis is at the North Pole, <u>Aurora Australis</u> is at the south - even though you almost never see it from Australia!

particles from their sun interact with it to form the incredible auroras here, just like on Earth and Jupiter."

"Wow," Chase muttered. He caught himself wondering, *does knowing all this science make it less beautiful, or more? Perhaps it doesn't matter – it looks simply amazing!*

"Sadly, in a few million years the magnetism will tear this planet apart and it'll all be gone," she said, frowning.

They looked at the sky outside the Auroran Lookout, for a good hour, silently watching the shifting shades of green and orange and blue. Chase sat on the ground and just stared until his eyes began to dry out and he had to blink repeatedly to stop them from hurting.

"Come," Moiya offered, "let us watch from inside."

Chapter 8
How *not* to make friends in the Universal Unity

Moiya then showed them the Auroran hotel where they stayed for the rest of the day, eating for free because they were guests, and guests always ate for free in the worlds of the Universal Unity, it was *actually* a law! Chase found it easy to relax, and he noticed the heat, gravity and air pressure were very much like a warm day on Earth.

Over the rest of the day Moiya came and went as he pleased, always turning up just when he was needed. He was happy to help translate for them or to tell them about Rlaeiul and its long history, especially about the one and only war they'd ever had. It turned out that Moiya started learning English in his sleep about two Earth years ago. At first his parents were worried that something was wrong with him but then they just decided it had something to do with his intuition and left him to it. Chase was very glad to have Moiya to talk to!

Arren tried to trade some of the old Coebri gear, but the Rlaeiulians seemed to have pretty much everything they already wanted. Instead, they stocked her cupboards with fresh fruit and water for free. She tried to give them some gold nuggets in thanks but they didn't want anything. In the end, Lucky got Arren to put a hole in an old fifty cent piece he had been carrying around in his backpack and gave that to Moiya to put on his necklace as a gesture of gratitude. It seemed to be just what the Rlaeiulians expected, Moiya was almost in tears of gratitude and showed it to everyone he met.

Chased loved Rlaeiul. The lights of the aurora never died down, and were their brightest at night. The darkness came quickly on Rlaeiul and the stars were never far away – many of the brightest were there all day. Chase just loved to walk in the perpetual world of blue and stare out at the never-quite-night sky to admire the aurora or the blue supergiant planet that Rlaeiul orbited. It was, in many ways, looking like it was going to be a very pleasant stay... until that evening when something unexpected happened.

It all started when Lucky did a magic trick. The Rlaeiulians were very impressed and made him do it again and again.

"Don't get out much, do they?" Lucky said as they nattered among themselves, trying to work it out.

"Probably because it takes visitors so long to acclimatise to the conditions," Chase said, and went to bed thinking nothing of it. They slept on wonderfully soft beds made from fur and feathers.

The next morning, another twenty smiling Rlaeiulians were waiting outside Lucky's door, waiting to see the magic trick.

Of course he showed them...

And by lunchtime, when they were heading for the pool, there were over fifty.

"I don't think I like the look of where this is heading..." Arren said, brow furrowed.

"Go on," Chase joked, "They love it, look at them!"

The Rlaeiulians were applauding again and Lucky sat down next to them by the deck.

"Ahh, the life of a celebrity!" He smirked.

"You don't suppose this is going to get out of hand?" Arren suggested, looking at the dozens of impressionable Rlaeiulians pressing their noses to the hotel glass to get a glimpse of Lucky. There were quite a few young females among them.

"Quit your worrying Arren, what harm can it do?" He smirked.

She didn't answer.

But by dinner time, there were over six hundred. They were pushing at the hotel glass trying to get a look at Lucky. They unintentionally crushed the pot plants at the entrance and one of them accidentally cut the hotel manager's arm while trying to get Lucky's autograph. The manager called in extra help at the hotel but it only seemed to spread the word even more.

By that time Arren and Chase were keeping a low profile in the lounge, and Lucky was nowhere to be found.

Moiya came in wearing his strange gas mask which looked like a leaf tied on by string. As usual he seemed uncomfortable in all the extra gravity.

"Where is Lucky?" He asked, trying to stretch up straight.

Arren shrugged, flipping casually though the pages in a magazine. "He's hiding," she said, fed up with him.

"Where?" Moiya asked, "The people are asking for him."

"Oh, you worry too much," Arren said, mocking his voice. "Let's just throw him to them and see what happens!" She joked.

"Arren!" Chase smiled, "Come on, let's go find him." He knew his brother had a way of getting into situations he couldn't handle. They went up to their room but he didn't seem to be there either.

"You don't suppose he's already slipped out?" Chase asked.

"Oh no, they'd know if he did," Moiya said. Chase didn't doubt him.

Arren opened up the cupboards, then she flipped open the draws. "Lucky, your fans are waiting! Yoo hoo, Lucky!" She said, pretending to look for him inside the mirror.

"I don't think he's in here," Chase finally decided.

Then Moiya showed a hint of a smile. Kneeling down with great effort he looked under the bed. It was a terribly laboured sight; the tall, lanky blue humanoid stretching against much more gravity than he was used to.

Lucky's disappointed voice shot out from under the bed.

"D'oh. Curse you and your intuition!" He exclaimed, crawling out and standing up. "Are they gone yet?" He asked.

They all shook their heads.

"Blast! Who'd a thought a little magic…" He peeked out the window but shut it quickly. "There must be a thousand of them now! We can't even get out of the hotel," he said in exasperation.

"I thought you *liked* the attention?" Arren teased him, smiling.

"I do, but *this* is ridiculous! Can't we just leave?" He begged her.

"Well, that didn't last long," Chase muttered.

She sighed. "I can try phasing the ship right into the hotel, or we can climb on the roof."

"Oh no," Moiya disagreed, "They'll know if you're planning to run onto the roof."

"Yeah, forgot that…" muttered Arren, "Well, we can always wait a week for them to go away?"

"Aarrh!" Lucky said in desperation. "Hey, Moiya, can you do me a favour? Can you tell them all that I'm out? Just pop down there and tell them we've left already, that way we can slip out safe–"

He never did finish, as that was when Moiya let out a tremendous wail of grief.

"Lies! Lies!" He panicked. "He asked me to lie!"

"Hey, it's not like that buddy…" Lucky tried to say, but Moiya was out the door.

"What just happened?" Lucky asked.

"I don't know," Arren said, scratching her head in confusion.

"You just asked Moiya to lie for you," Chase explained.

For a moment there was silence.

"Get your stuff," Arren ordered, her voice tense, her smile gone.

"What, what's the matter?" Lucky said, still confused.

She grabbed their suits and bags, helping them to pull them on as quickly as they could.

"I *told* you Lucky," Arren almost shouted. "I *told* you! These people hate lies! Now what will we do?"

They donned their spacesuits, stuffed their belongings in the backpacks and shoved on their helmets.

"How close is the ship?" Chase asked.

"I'm flying it in now but it's still a bit too far."

"What's happening out there?" Chase said, peering out the window.

Arren peeped down. Watching from above she seemed to be reading their lips.

"It seems there's an old elder there. One who remembers the war. He's… he's really angry. He's getting them really worked up. That's not like the Universal Unity at all! The girls, they're *setting fire* to the posters they made of you Lucky! He's telling them you need to be … your lies need to be cleansed in the fire of their sun!"

"They're what?! They're nuts, that's what they are!"

"They're certainly not behaving how I'd expect Rlaeiulians to," Arren agreed.

"It was just one little lie and we didn't even say it! Oh, what do we do now?" Lucky moaned.

Arren was squinting out the window when she saw something that really freaked her out.

"Run!" she squealed.

They had only gone a few paces towards the door when the hotel suddenly lost pressure; the ex-fans had broken in and were on the hunt for Lucky. A second later they heard voices from down the hall, and a moment after that a dozen blue, angry and very tall humanoids stumbled down the corridor carrying pitchforks and torches.

"Where did they get those?!" Lucky screamed in disbelief.

Someone shouted something like 'there they are!' and started stumbling towards them, straining against the gravity[36].

The three of them ran up a flight of stairs towards the roof exit. Lucky banged on the door to get out.

"Get out of the way!" Arren yelled, and putting her hand on a panel beside the door it slowly began to change. "It's heat sensitive!"

The angry mob was approaching.

They were only a dozen meters away. One of them tried to hurl his pitchfork but it fell at his own feet. He stared at it in disappointment.

"Guess they aren't used to Earth gravity," Lucky grinned.

"We need more time," Arren shouted.

Chase watched them struggle at the foot of the stairs and thought of a clever idea.

---

[36] Just to clarify; a change in pressure has no effect on gravity. Just because the hotel lost air pressure doesn't mean people start to float!

"Look out behind you!" he yelled, looking worried and pointing at the wall behind the mob.

They just weren't used to people lying. In spite of their possibly murderous intent towards Lucky, they all turned around in alarm and in their haste, fell over each other. In a moment they were a large, tangled pile of struggling blue limbs and pitchforks. Their faint torches went out quickly in the weak atmosphere.

"Let's go," Arren shouted. She shoved open the door...

... and there was Moiya.

For a moment, they looked at each other in silence.

"I think you'd better leave," he whispered.

"I know," said Chase, slipping by him.

"There," shouted Arren. Her ship rose up from the ground as though it had taken a short cut through the centre of Rlaeiul.

"Quickly, they are coming!" Moiya said in alarm. A moment later a pair of adult Rlaeiulians got to their feet at the base of the stairs.

"Run," Arren shouted, sprinting away.

"Moiya, I'm, I'm sorry," Lucky said.

Moiya smiled. "I know."

"Come on!" Chase said, grabbing his bother. Lucky and Chase had a head start but the Rlaeiulians were insanely fast on their long legs once they got out of the hotel.

"Jump!" Lucky shouted, mid-stride.

"What?" Chase asked.

Then he saw it; Arren's ship was still quite a distance from the edge of the balcony. Fortunately they could leap incredibly far in Rlaeiuian gravity.

They jumped.

Arren was first, sailing in calmly and spinning around at the door to help them in.

Lucky was second, laughing crazily the whole way.

Chase was third, eyes screwed shut, screaming every inch of the way. He hit the padded deck of the air lock with a thunderous *crash*. An instant later Arren wrenched the door shut and there was a mysterious thud as an enraged Rlaeiulian fell against the ship.

"OK, I think we've seen enough of Rlaeiul for now, boys?" She suggested.

"I *really* prefer Cambriania," Lucky said, hopping from one foot to the other while trying to get the spacesuit off extra quick.

"You got us in so much… Why *are* you hopping around like that?" Arren asked him.

"I gotta pee!" he shouted, and took off down the corridor.

"What *are* we going to do with him?" Arren sighed.

Chapter 9
Tauroo

Chase wandered onto the control deck, feeling a bit sad. The Rlaeiulians were some of the nicest people he'd ever met, generous, quiet and blue. So very, very blue. It was a terrible way to leave such nice people. Lucky had gone off to mope, trying to work out the ship's strange geography again. He was avoiding Arren.

Chase sighed.

"Miss 'em already?" Arren said. She was watching the stars in the control room, lying down on the deck with nothing but a giant python and a forgotten fence paling to keep her company.

He nodded and sat beside her to look at the stars.

"I thought you might like it there," she said.

"So, where to now?" Chase asked.

"You sound so sad," Arren said, "Here, let's go somewhere that there's no higher intelligent beings around to accidentally upset, somewhere peaceful and quiet, where nothing can go wrong. A wilderness preserve planet, a little place I've wanted to see for years. Might cheer you up? Want to see Tauroo?"

He nodded and the screens switched to a view of a beautiful orange gas giant with short rings, a little like Saturn.

"What is that?" Chase asked.

She laughed, "It's Tauroo. We're going to take a little look around."

Suddenly all the screens turned off. "But I want this to be a surprise. Now, I'm going to stop the ship at a point where, believe it or not, the air pressure is exactly the same as it is back on Earth. So you won't need to wear the suits. The air composition, however, is just a little different. So, before we leave I'll need you and Lucky to take a little drink of some water I'll make. It will temporarily alter your body chemistry so that you can feel comfortable in this atmosphere. OK?"

"OK!" Chase agreed. He was beginning to like the idea of experimenting on anything she handed him, especially if it meant the chance to explore another world. "Come on, let's go find Lucky."

As it was, Arren had talked to him over the intercom already and he was waiting at the entry for them.

"Hey… sorry, about… you know," he stumbled to say to them.

"S'Ok," Chase said.

"Don't worry about it, forget it." Arren smiled.

They toasted each other with the little paper cups she gave them to drink from, then she swung open the door.

Outside it looked like they were on top of a mountain, but in fact there was nothing underneath them except for more and more air, as far down as it was possible to lean out and see. The sky was a sapphire blue and filled with incredibly tall clouds of orange and white. At first, Chase thought the air outside smelt a bit strange but he got used to it pretty quick.

"Wow." Lucky's words mirrored Chase's thoughts.

Arren laughed. "You guys impressed?"

They nodded and took a step out the door and onto the deck of Arren's ship. Arren quickly clipped a safety lead onto her torso harness, which she wore constantly over her space suit, at least when they weren't on Earth. She held up some safety leads for them to wear too, but they didn't even have belts to strap them on. She shrugged to herself, and spoke a warning instead to Lucky who dared to stand right on the edge of the deck.

"Don't go over the edge," she told him. "I'm negating some of the gravity here and you will not enjoy the unexpected increase if you start falling faster than you ever knew was possible, let me assure you!"

Chase looked out at the clouds which just seemed to go on forever and ever. They were every colour of orange and white and pink. Then he noticed, floating through one of those clouds, a strange balloon thing with a tussle of hair on top and writhing tentacles underneath. At first he thought it might have been a strange alien device or something but then he noticed it looked alive...

"Right on time," Arren smiled.

"What is it?" Chase asked.

"One of the residents of Tauroo," Arren said. "Sky based life forms. Most of them use gas bladders to make themselves less dense than the surrounding air[37]. They spend their entire lives floating around, never landing anywhere because there is nowhere to land."

"They're living blimps?" Lucky asked.

"Exactly." She smiled.

"Are there - whoa!" Lucky started, and then pointed to where a huge flock of living blimps were floating their way.

There where thousands of them, all different sizes. Most of them passed around the ship, but a few curious ones moved in close and reached out to them with their

---

[36] Lots of sea animals on earth use <u>gas bladders</u> – a special organ that can fill with air to help them keep balance and float without physical effort. But these animals I made up: imagine a gas bladder full of something like hydrogen gas. The animal might, if the rest of it was light enough, be able to float through the air! Still, no air-floating animals of this kind are known to exist in nature.

tentacles. Chase touched one, it felt a bit like a felt-covered snake.

"How smart are they?" he wondered out loud.

"About as smart as birds," she said, "Though some of the larger ones are as smart as whales and dolphins. They've been here for a very long time. Would you like me to send out an ultrasonic invitation to see if I can get one of the larger ones to say hello?"

"Yes please!" he replied.

Just then a flock of little blimps shot past, propelled by flitting bat-like wings and chirping like birds. They were blimp birds and the air was full of their strange songs.

"They like strangers," Arren said, her voice quiet.

"What... what do they eat?" Lucky asked in wonder.

Chase couldn't believe his brother had asked that question, like there was a hidden scientific side to him as well. Oh, hang on; it was a question about *food*.

"Little mites smaller than dust," Arren replied. "They filter them out of the air. This whole planet's ecosystem relies on them."

Just then several of the larger blimps scattered as a large spear fell from the clouds, opened up and reinflated into another strange blimp with sharp spines on its tentacles, fins spinning like propellers to help it slow its fall.

"And the meat eaters. They impale the other blimps for food."

"Really?" Chase asked, fascinated.

"And, ooh!" Arren began, but stopped in amazement as a great behemoth of a blimp split the clouds down beneath them and emerged from within a sea of white fog. It had orange and brown stripes down its side and the meat eaters fled as soon as it arrived, but the other blimp beings didn't seem to mind. It was huge, as big as a blue whale. It turned side on and there they could see the unmistakable sight of an eye looking right at them. An eye as large as football. For a moment Chase was speechless as the behemoth-like being floated closer with its huge fins of waving ribbons.

"That's *huge*," Lucky muttered.

"He won't stay here long," Arren explained, "The air pressure is too low and he's much more comfortable deeper down. Hello Taurioon!" She waved.

They watched as the whale-blimp slowly floated by.

"So let me see if I've got this," Lucky said, "Air is made up of tiny little bouncing balls, bouncing all the time and that's what creates pressure. And that pressure is about a kilogram on a space the size of your fingernail, or as much as a car over your whole body. That's so much it can blow you right out of the door of a space ship–"

"– Or lift the roof off in a storm, or push you into a tornado. Air doesn't suck, it only pushes," she interrupted.

"Yes, all that. And liquids are just gasses under pressure, so if you remove pressure, all your body's liquids turn into gasses and you'll explode."

"More or less," she said.

He nodded. "And now you're telling me that the further *down* you go, the *more* pressure there is? Why?"

"Because the further down you go, the more air there is above you, pushing down on you. High pressure at the bottom, lower pressure at the top[38]."

---

[37] Another interesting effect of air pressure is on the boiling point of water. At low pressures, like at the top of mountains, water boils at lower temperatures – so it takes a little longer to cook anything! In an area of high pressure, like in a pressure cooker, the water can get really hot, well above a hundred degrees centigrade, and still not be boiling!

"So why don't I feel any air pressure now?" he asked.

"You're taking it for granted because it's been there your whole life, keeping you alive. But you notice air pressure when it suddenly changes[39], like when you drive up a hill or jump out of an aeroplane."

"So high pressure down low, low pressure up high?"

"That's right!" She gave him an approving smile. "Though you can create high pressure in other ways; heating the air up causes higher pressure too."

"Yeah, so... if there was no pressure we could float right?" Lucky said.

She slapped her forehead in frustration. "No, pressure has nothing to do with whether you can float or not. That's just gravity.[40]"

"What I want to know," Chase then asked, "is who came up with all this idea of air pressure. Who thinks this kind of thing up?"

Arren laughed, but got very excited, "I'm *so glad* you asked! Behind every single science idea ever, *ever*, there is a *someone*. A *person* had to think of the idea; science ideas don't just drop out the sky and into your science books. *Someone* came up with the idea, and they had to have a pretty good reason why. And when it comes to air pressure some of the credit has to go to Evangelista Torricelli, another Italian like Ms Garibaldi, don't ya know?"

"No I didn't," Lucky muttered, looking out at the clouds.

---

[39] For example, when you drive up a steep hill there's less air the higher up you go, so there are less little particles bouncing against you. But the air inside your ears hasn't had time to change, so the air inside will push harder than the air outside and that makes your ear drums stretch out, and it hurts your head right? Ever felt like that? And same thing going down except the air pushes in more than out.

[40] See, told you.

"Well, back in sixteen forty three, Torricelli was trying to work out why a mine was having trouble pumping water out when the water had to go up over ten meters. He figured out it was the air pushing down on the water that pushed it up the pipe, not the pump *pulling* the water up at all! He invented the first barometer in the process, and realised it changed with the weather and so could be used to help predict it. Clever guy, he started a big debate about infinity using a trumpet, and is famous for writing in a letter to Michelangelo "Noi viviamo sommersi nel fondo d'un pelago d'aria[41], which means–"

Lucky suddenly interrupted, "Hang on, can a sudden change in pressure do any damage to you personally?"

She stopped her lecture and answered, "Not usually, but in certain circumstances it might! For example, when coming up from a deep sea dive a sudden return to normal air pressure can cause the extra nitrogen in your blood to turn into gas bubbles, now *that's* painful. I believe you call it 'the bends' on Earth when it happens to deep sea divers who come up too quickly?"

"Yeah, I've heard of it," Chase agreed.

"And a sudden increase can press in on your body so much that, for example, your lungs collapse. So, no extreme changes in air pressure, right?"

"Right," Chase replied, then smiled. "You know, you're always ready with these little lessons, aren't you?"

She sighed, gazing out at the seemingly endless world of clouds. "I guess I just want you to know that the universe is a more wonderful place than you have ever imagined. And... that so much of what makes it amazing cannot be *seen*, only *understood*."

---

[41] "We live submerged at the bottom of an ocean of air."

Suddenly, with a mournful roar, the large behemoth-blimp turned away from them and began to speed away, as much as something as big as a whale can 'speed', anyway.

"What's up with him, I wonder?" Chase asked.

Suddenly Arren's ship gave a jolt downwards.

"What the…" Lucky cried in alarm.

"Oh, I wasn't paying attention, get back inside, quick!" Arren shouted.

"What, what's happening?" Chase complained, looking around, which in hindsight wasn't the smartest thing to do. He should just have run to the door like Lucky did. Instead he just *stood there*, looking around.

There, towards the far edge, a huge tentacle was wrapping itself around Arren's ship.

"A Leviathan!" Arren shouted.

The ship lurched again and Chase was thrown to the deck. He reached out instinctively to grab a pole but his grasping fingers fell short as the ship gave another sudden lurch downwards.

He fell screaming backwards, sliding across the hull and falling down into the blackness. For a moment he thought he was going to die. Then his body gave an unexpected jerk as something grabbed hold of his leg.

"Got you!" Arren called from up above.

Chase looked up to see a service spider standing on a crane arm. It had grabbed a hold of his leg, preventing him from plummeting into who-knew-what.

"Don't look down!" she insisted.

So, of course, Chase looked down. Instantly he was mesmerised by the scene below him. The clouds were billowing and black as something impossibly large and unfathomably dark stirred beneath them. Two spined and dark tentacles with large air sacs writhed up at least a kilometre from the turmoil to wrap themselves around Arren's ship.

"Can't you just disappear us?" Chase screamed.

"Not with you on the outside!" She shouted, as the spider desperately tried to help him up. It had a painfully firm grip on his leg and he felt much heavier, as if gravity had just doubled. He grabbed hold of the crane arm and pulled himself up with great difficulty. The crane turned around and helped him back onto the bottom edge of the ship.

Lucky was already at the door. Chase ran with Arren, stumbling as best as they could up the trembling hull.

"Hurry!" Lucky screamed, he seemed really worried, but his voice sounded muted and distant. That was when Chase realised his ears hurt. He instinctively opened his mouth wide to try and relieve the pressure build up. He felt the wind rushing against the back of his head and an incredible increase in pressure against his nose right between his eyes. He felt strange, like his head was in a vice and all the air was pressing in around him.

"We're falling," Arren shouted, though her voice was hard to hear in the confusion.

Still, thought Chase, *that would explain it*. The further they fell, the more the air pressure outside would increase. Then his ears and face really started to hurt and he got a huge headache. He began to wonder, *if the air pressure increased any more, would my face burst?*

"It's not the air pressure that's the problem!" Arren explained, seeming to guess his thoughts as they stumbled along, now on their knees to keep from falling off, while spiders stumbled along beside them or tried to tie down wildly swinging ladders and panels that had broken lose. "It's the air pressure *difference* between the inside and outside of your head. Try swallowing to open up your Eustachian tubes."

That was too much information, given the situation! He didn't have any idea what an Eustachian tube[42] was, but he swallowed anyway and his ears popped a little. Suddenly, the ship took another sudden jolt and he was thrown sideways. The air pressure increased dramatically.

"Ouch! He's charged like an electric eel! No one told me they had an electric charge. Right!" Arren said, and her ship pulled up hard against the leviathan's grip.

"Get inside!" she told him with clenched teeth.

Chase scrambled along the deck until Lucky was able to pull him inside and they collapsed on the floor, breathing heavily, almost squashing Lopi in the process. She hissed at them in annoyance.

---

[41] The Eustachian tube is a little tunnel that runs from our ears to the back of our throat and it is used to balance the air pressure inside and outside our heads. Next time your ears are hurting because of a change in pressure – driving down a hill or riding in an airplane – try balancing out the pressure by opening up your Eustachian tube through swallowing, chewing, yawning, blowing your nose, breathing gently into your nose while holding it closed, there's loads of options!

"Geez, do we end up running for our lives *everywhere* we go?" Lucky asked.

In the next moment, Arren flung herself in and started stumbling towards the control room. Her ship was still shaking, making strange groaning sounds.

"What's happening?!" Chase shouted.

"We're still falling," she called from up ahead, "That *thing* damaged the engines and the electric shock decalibrated my quantum teleporter. I can't even make us transparent again!"

They ran to the screens and looked at them in alarm. The air outside was growing darker and darker. They were plummeting into the unknown depths of a giant world made mostly of air.

"I'm not built for this kind of pressure..." Arren whimpered, curling up on her chair, her ship lurching in odd patterns through the sky as she engaged in some kind of invisible battle to bring it under control once more.

"Then get us out of here! Make a wormhole or something!"

"I can't, not inside a planetary atmosphere, it's too dangerous!"

"What's going to happen to us?" Chase asked.

"The air pressure will increase until the hull begins to crack. Then we'll crash into the sea that's in the middle of every gas giant. It'll be like hitting concrete."

There had to be another option, but they seemed pretty low on options right now, and Arren didn't seem to be thinking clearly with whatever the pressure was doing to her ship. Chase knew what to do: They were going to have to try and risk forming a wormhole to get their way out of there!

Then, suddenly, all the screens in the control room turned completely white.

"What … just … happened?" Lucky asked.

Arren looked confused, then sat back on her chair in resignation. "We, gentlemen, are *inside* a Nova Class high-end multidimensional Universal Unity star craft."

Chapter 10
Inside a Nova Class high-end multidimensional Universal Unity Star craft

Chase pressed his nose up to the screens, trying to make out faint details in the blinding light outside. Slowly the scene began to clear and it looked like they were in some kind of futuristic city, floating above golden streets with perfect rows of healthy looking fruit trees. Dozens of creatures of every race imaginable walked or strolled around in clothes of white or pearl or pale blue. They didn't seem at all alarmed by the asteroid mining monstrosity that had been forcibly materialised into the middle of their central plaza. Everything else was clean and neat and looked like it was built to last forever. It was the most breathtaking city Chase had ever seen.

Lucky looked down his nose at all the neatness. "I still prefer Cambriania," he muttered.

As Chase watched he noticed about a dozen creatures walking towards their ship in a very military fashion. They were a bizarre array of wildly different species. Some had feathers, others tentacles. One even looked like a floating fish. They were dressed like soldiers, wearing black and silver army dress uniforms, neat and well pressed with forward peaked caps. At their side, they had batons. Their leader was an important looking woman, glaring right up at the screen as though she could see him looking out at her.

A moment later, the dozen creatures simply appeared on the deck.

Do people everywhere seem to know how to do that, except for Earth? Chase wondered.

"Hello children, you are a long way from home," the important looking woman said. She looked human, and her voice was business-like and professional, but with a touch of kindness. Like a psychologist.

Chase and his friends stood on the raised platform where Arren's pilot chair was, while the lady and her guards waited in readiness on the deck. One of them, a strange looking man who seemed to be made out of stone, tried to walk onto the platform.

"Leave us alone!" Lucky shouted, and picked up his fence paling. He took a warning swipe in a last-ditch act of defiance.

The guards all gasped and leapt back. Except their leader, she just stood there surveying the scene in complete calm.

"Come up here and we'll clobber you!" Lucky shouted. Chase could tell he wasn't really mad, he was just stalling for time until they thought of more options.

"Lucky, be careful," Arren warned with concern in her voice. She obviously did not know Lucky was bluffing. Neither, Chase realised, would the guards.

Then the man he'd taken a swipe at got a determined look on his face and with one unbelievably swift move, managed to dodge Lucky and grab him, pinning his arms to his side and lifting him off the deck at arm's length.

He must have been very strong.

"Hey, put me down or else!" Lucky roared.

"Stop struggling, you may hurt yourself," the man stated in a bored voice like it was a maths fact or something. But Chase thought he could hear a little fear underneath that bravado.

Then Lucky kicked him in the left shin, hard.

Everyone gasped and the man dropped Lucky and limped back. Two of his friends held him up, seeming very concerned. One of them gave Lucky a 'how could you do that!' kind of look. The kicked man tried to hold his head up proud, but then he bit down on his finger as if to keep from bursting into tears.

"Violence..." one of them muttered in awe.

The mood in the room went from tense, to warlike.

"Ahh, Lucky, I think you should get back here," Chase suggested.

Lucky took a step back while everyone else stood still, wondering what to do. Then a different woman guard walked up to him, pointed a webbed, red finger at his forehead and ordered, "Drop your weapon!"

It felt like a gentle breeze mysteriously brushed passed Lucky and on to Chase, and everyone was silent for a moment.

Then Lucky just laughed.

The guards gasped and jumped back like they had seen a miracle.

"What, what's the problem guys!" Lucky mocked them. "Afraid of a little Earthling! Bring it freaks, bring it–"

He didn't finish, as suddenly the important looking woman said, "Enough!"

Reaching out, a baton materialised into her hand and with one of the most gentle slaps Chase had ever seen, landed one right on the back of Lucky's knee.

With a yell he hit the deck, writhing in pain. Chase dragged him back on the platform.

"What on earth have you got in that thing?!" Lucky demanded to know.

"Whatever I want," the lady replied, and showed them a ring of blue lightning that crackled up the baton. "You think you're the only ones born outside the Unity around here? Ha! And *you*," she said, in a firm but gentle voice to Arren, "Have been a very naughty little class two research and reclamation vessel." And she gave a little smile while she waved a 'naughty, naughty' finger at her.

Arren returned half a smile. "I suppose, then, that you've come to take me back to the Coebri?" Arren replied with a hint of resignation in her voice.

"Oh no, nothing of the sort." The lady smiled.

Arren cocked her head. "Then why are you doing this?"

Chase helped Lucky to his feet. At the same time the man he kicked pushed away his proud admirers. They acted like this was the first time any of them had ever been kicked in the shins, or witnessed any kind of violence. Except for the lady, she seemed a lot more experienced than the rest. But Chase had to wonder if the wounded soldier was going to be a hero in his world for years for facing off against the insane and violent 'Lucky of planet Earth'.

The lady smiled. "You think we've got nothing better to do than chase around missing Coebri property? Let them do their own dirty work! We are quite happy for you and the others to escape. Do you think you find it so easy to hack into our universal internet just because you're clever? No. We *want* you to know about the rest of the universe. We know you are meant for something more than digging out asteroids day in, day out."

Arren shifted uncomfortably. "Then why all this? Why this... show of force?"

"Well," the lady began, "We still have laws to keep, and a fragile alliance with the Coebri and others. Why else do you think we sent a tracker after you? You were supposed to destroy him, but you didn't. That would have made it nice and easy to get us out of our legal obligations. We fully expected you to head to somewhere neutral like Cambriania; we could have spent your entire life time caught up in legalities without ever spoiling your holiday. But instead, you had to go to Earth. Lonely, violent Earth. And then you took two of them with you, for heaven's sake?! What were you thinking?"

"I... I... you *wanted* me to destroy the tracker?" Arren almost shouted, distracted by what the lady had said.

"Indeed, Arren. That is what these boys call you, isn't it?"

"We're right here," Lucky muttered.

"Yes, sorry, you're quite right. Sorry again."

"Yes, my name is Arren now. They call me Arren," she said, folding her arms in protest.

"So what happens now?" Chase asked.

The lady waited a moment before explaining to him, "She's been apprehended by a Universal Unity vessel. There's only one thing we can do. We have to take her back to the Coebri, where they will fit her with a slave collar and she'll never be able to leave again. You do know how long she will live, don't you? Then we will take you back to Earth and forcibly erase your whole memory of this event. I'm sorry, but that's just the way it has to be."

"What?! NO!" Chase yelled.

The lady stood her ground and Chase was within arm's reach of her stunning baton but the guards jumped back like he'd hit them all with something.

They aren't very good guards, he found himself thinking.

"I'm sorry," she said, without smiling. "I have no other legal options."

"Yes, yes you do," Chase disagreed, "I claimed this ship when it landed on my world. It's mine now!"

If he expected a fight, or at least some surprise, he was disappointed. Instead the lady looked over at Arren and seemed sad.

"What have you done, little Arren?" Then she looked at Chase. She wasn't at all like the guards. She acted like the people he knew, not intimidated. "She hasn't told you, has she?"

"No!" Arren begged, and leapt out of her chair to press herself up against the banister, pushing her pleading face right up to the lady's.

"You didn't tell them?" The lady repeated.

"Tell me what?" Chase said, never realising till much later he'd just asked exactly what the lady wanted him to.

"No," Arren repeated, looking at him, sorrow written all over her face.

"He deserves to know," the lady said, "He *needs* to know."

"No, no, no, no! Oh, I was going to tell you! I was *trying* to tell you!"

"Tell us what?" Lucky demanded. His voice was flat and unkind, and Chase finally realised; Lucky did not trust Arren, he never had.

"I didn't lie," she apologised, swiping her hand around as if to chase away the approaching revelation.

"Among our people, Arren, allowing someone to believe a lie is as good as lying. You know this," the lady taught.

Again, Arren was tearing up. "I... I...."

Then Chase realised she'd been lying to him about something, or keeping something from them that they needed to know. Perhaps she was a criminal, or a thief? Perhaps...

"What is it Arren?" He said coldly.

She stuttered like she didn't know what to say.

"Chase," the lady said, "Arren *is* this ship."

"What?" He said, not understanding. At least she wasn't a criminal... maybe?

Through her tears, Arren tried to explain, "I'm not just bioneurologically connected to this ship. I am a... a manifestation of it. You know those spiders? They're... they're me too. I'm this ship and this human form body was something I created to help me explore this universe. But I'm alive. I have a soul, I have a soul!" She shouted, jabbing a pointed finger at the lady as if to dare her to disagree. The entire ship shuddered, as though it shared the depths of her feelings.

"Indeed you do," the lady replied, "And you are just as capable of lying, stealing and making mistakes as any other living, sentient being."

Now Arren was crying.

Chase went up to her then and held her arm. It was warm. It felt like human flesh.

"It's a bioresin polymer around a calcium lined metalloid skeleton. I use a subspace link to transfer information from me to this body but it can still function without it. *I* can function without it. I'm *alive* Chase, you have to believe me. I am alive!" And for just a moment her voice seemed to echo throughout every corridor and room of the immense space ship.

Chase didn't know what to think.

So Arren wasn't a human. She wasn't a girl. She wasn't even a person. She was the entire ship, full of little interconnected machines. And one of them looked like a girl. And talked like a girl. And burst into tears at the thought of going back to being a slave again.

"No," he stated firmly.

Arren pleaded, "Chase..." she said, looking like she was about to lose her only friend.

"No!" He shouted, tearing away from her. So she wasn't what he thought she was? *So what.* "I don't care if she's not human, or if this whole ship is her. You can't take her back to slavery!"

The lady seemed surprised.

Arren smiled broadly.

The guards gasped – was it fear, or admiration?

"I don't care what she is, she doesn't deserve to live in fear! And I don't care what she's done, it can't be bad enough to force her back to those *pirates!*"

The lady looked severe. "You can't just go breaking our laws, Earthling. We have you and your ship caught in a multidimensional parallelity, warded against all forms of mechanical breaching, quantum teleportation and what you people call 'wormholes'. Just *how* do you propose to take her away?"

Then Chase had a thought.

The kind of thought these people would have *never* had.

He snatched the fence paling from his brother and grabbed the lady by the arm. Shouting at the top of his lungs he declared.

"Let us go or I will wack her with this stick!"

The guards gasped in horror.

"Do as he says," the lady stated, sounding not in the least bit worried. Almost as if she'd expected it. "There's *nothing* we can do now."

The guards hesitated but she nodded them on and they disappeared one by one. For an advanced alien species, they seemed a little low on options against an Earthling wielding a stick.

Arren's ship, or was it Arren herself, quickly floated out through the other ship's hull, preparing to leave.

"You need to get back to Earth," the lady whispered, smiling just a little. "You must stay hidden there. You cannot return to Unity space without us being required to apprehend you regardless of our personal beliefs. Also, there will be bounty hunters. Take care young ones. And Arren, don't forget the *Sosphira*."

Then, without any warning, she disappeared out of his grasp. A moment later, the star screens went into high speed.

"They *let us go*," Lucky stated, arms folded, his voice angry.

Chapter 11
When now you know what it was you never knew you never knew

For a long time there was silence.

Then Lucky spoke. "I *knew* it," he stated, "I knew it all along that there was something about you, *Arren*. You hear me?" He shouted at the walls.

"I hear you," she said.

He walked up and patted the barrier around the pilot's chair. "Oh look, I'm patting Arren!" He teased.

Then he touched the wall. "Look, I'm touching Arren!"

Then he stomped on the floor. "Oops, I stepped on Arren!"

She sobbed softly. "That's just what the Coebri used to do."

Chase looked at Lucky and gave him a look that said 'shut up and don't be such an insensitive git'. Then he went up and patted her shoulder, her human form shoulder.

"Don't worry about him," Chase said.

Lucky was still indignant. "Don't worr – Arren, you lied to us! You got us to run all around the universe risking our lives for you and you didn't even have the courage to tell us you're just a machine!"

"A machine that *feels*," she whispered, eyes wet with whatever it was she used for tears.

It put him in his place, a little.

Chase smiled. "Look at it this way, Lucky. We didn't steal a car, we rescued a slave. That makes us heroes."

Lucky twisted his foot on the ground. "Yeah, I guess. It's been an intense day. And … and I think those guard wannabes kinda freaked me out. S...Sorry Arren."

She made him wait a few seconds before replying, "That's OK. I should have told you much sooner."

"What kind of people are they?" Lucky asked about the guards.

"Those that have never known violence. Not them, not their parents, not their great, great whatever grandparents. It's not part of their world, or their culture. Oh, they have competitions, but they don't get angry. Not like Earthlings do. You really freaked them out you know. They're terrified of you. Nothing they have stopped you."

"Then that's why," Lucky concluded, "That's why they keep us from their technologies. We'd dominate them all in a week."

"No," Arren said, angry at first, then quiet. "Not quite. But close enough..."

She looked at them then, as if she was deciding whether or not to do something important. Finally she made up her mind and said, "Come, there's something I'd like you to see."

She walked up to the back of the raised platform where the pilot's chair was and breathed on the wall. A second later there was a small hiss and a door shaped bulge appeared in the wall.

"What I have to show you is very sacred," she explained, "And delicate. Try not to think too many violent thoughts, will you?" She said, looking at Lucky.

"What're you looking at me for?" He protested.

Chase rolled his eyes as if to say 'you've got to be joking', and Arren did the same thing.

"Yeah, you're right," he said, frowning down his eyes in an insincere gesture of regret.

Arren took a deep breath.

"Only Tzaarkh, my father, has been in here, obviously. Here. Let me show you what I *really* am."

Chase found himself wondering what made that fact obvious, but let the matter drop as the portal popped open. Inside there was a huge spherical room, covered with so many little lights that it was impossible to tell exactly how large it was. The only place to stand was the narrow platform where they came in, a soft metal banister keeping them from falling down into the room. The walls and floor were so perfectly covered in stars that he seemed to be staring into the bottomless fathoms of space.

And there, floating about twenty meters away in what might have been the centre, was a collection of light. It looked ethereal, like translucent sheets of multi-coloured silk all curled up and held together by gossamer pins of pure light. It seemed to wave and flow with Arren's words and feelings.

She stood between them, then floated herself up off the platform and towards the ever shifting collection of lights.

"Ooh, pretty," Lucky mused.

"What... is it?" Chase asked, the curiosity almost exploding out of him.

"It's a polydimentional, infinite nanocalculator in subspace."

"Huh?" Lucky asked.

"A supercomputer made from space itself – the highest possible expression of the computer. It can perform an infinite number of calculations, all outside time so that it happens almost instantaneously. That's a rough translation anyway. And... it's me."

That was when it all made sense to Chase. When the ship was hurting, Arren was hurt, and when the ship needed rest, she felt tired. And when the ship had needed to shut down Arren had fainted. She wasn't controlling the ship, she was, what did she say, an "expression" of it. She was a spaceship, and she was exploring the universe.

"You're, you're that?" Lucky asked, disbelieving.

"Pretty much. I was built by the Coebri long ago. I started here and worked my way up, the Coebri adding whatever they thought was useful – rockets, transport bays etcetera. They connected in the spiders and the mining machines and I had to organise them all. I've spent over eight hundred years in this room, just thinking, adding numbers, preparing forged tax returns. Then one day about twelve years ago, I finally made a decision..."

She floated back down to them, close enough to be in arms reach.

"I had a wealth of knowledge but almost no experience. I could see the whole universe from my internet but I'd never seen it with my own eyes, or touched it with my own hands," she said, putting her hands out in front of her.

"So I made me. I made this body. It's taken twelve years to build and it's still growing. I'm still growing. Before, I could sense; now, I can feel. Before, I could know; now, I can understand."

"So, you're just like a human?" Chase asked.

"No, not at all! You're so *lucky* to be a human!" She said.

"Human?" Lucky disbelieved.

"Yes, Human! I know I'm always picking on Earthlings, but that's only because you have so much *potential*. I might be able to experience things but it's still not quite the same. Besides, I'm limited in other ways too. I can never be more than I've been programmed to be and even though that's a lot, I can't create things better than myself. Humans are *amazing*. You can go beyond your original programming to become whatever you want! As a race, you are unlimited. You have so much *choice*! Even when all the odds are stacked against you, you can still choose anything you want. And you are so *creative*. It's one of the things that rank you among the most powerful species in the universe."

"I'd never thought of that," Chase admitted.

"I do like choosing," Lucky said, "Or rather, doing whatever I want!"

She laughed. "That doesn't mean you can escape the consequences of your choices. No one can. But humans are amazing. They change everything they touch. They feel, and they know, and they can become something so wonderful! I'm just a class two research and reclamation vessel…"

"But, you're amazing too!" Chase argued. "You can speak any language you want, you can fly anywhere around space, you, you know so much and can fix *anything*! I'd *love* to know how to do that."

"Yeah, but you're *human*," she repeated with a longing sigh.

"Oh, it's not all that great," Lucky said, getting serious all of a sudden. "We keep making mistakes and doing dumb things. Like, I'm always getting in trouble for disobeying teachers, can't ever seem to sit still. I'm just the class freak."

"Yeah," Chase said, picking up on the self-berating, "And I'm, well, a science geek. I'm always getting picked on and never do anything about it. And I don't tell anyone what I'm feeling because if I do… I … might burst into tears," he confessed.

Lucky looked surprised at that confession, like he'd never really thought about it.

"What?" Arren said, floating closer. "No, no, no, no. Don't you see? You're both perfect. Perfect *just* the way you are. Even with all your weaknesses. Lucky, you think you're fidgety but you have so much energy, and it's one of your gifts to the world. And Chase, you're clever and sensitive. You keep people out but that's only because you care so much about making the world a better place. You're both perfect just the way you are!"

There wasn't anything to be said about that, so they said nothing.

A moment of understanding passed between them.

"Thanks Arren," Chase said.

She smiled and held out her hand. He touched it again. It was smooth and soft. It looked pretty human to him.

"Ahh, well, if you two are just going to hold hands in here I suppose I'd better leave," Lucky teased them.

Chase pulled his hand away pretty quick. "It's not like that. I was examining her hand ... for scientific purposes," he argued.

"Oh, I think it's *exactly* like that." Lucky smirked.

Chase felt his face flush hot and he lost the words to reply.

Arren laughed. "I like you guys. Even if I wasn't running for my life from the Coebri, I'd be glad if I ran into you guys."

"Thanks Arren," Lucky replied. Then he sighed. "So... like Chase is always saying, what happens now?"

Arren looked at the stars around her. "Let's get you guys home. I want to make a proper entry this time. One and a half hours, no comet trail, no crashing into the ground. I'm going to land in Ms Garibaldi's yard and then we're going to figure out what happens next."

"What does happen next?" Chase wondered.

"Let's get you guys a sonic shower and sunbath. Then a change of clothes and maybe some dinner."

"Cool!" Lucky said.

They took it easy and had dinner in Arren's garden, lit by the blazing blue light of a supergiant sun that Earth had never seen or named. Then they popped back into their normal solar system and Arren showed them what it was like to look on their world from outer space.

It was blue and white and very beautiful in every way. Chase was speechless as they watched it grow as they flew closer. Lucky tried to make out the outlines of countries and famous landmarks like the Great Wall of China, but it seemed harder than he had expected. Chase thought the night side of the Earth was the most amazing, with countless cities like stars in the night, and the lightning from the storms across the world never really stopped.

To Chase, his world looked so large and powerful, but also so very gentle, almost … delicate. Like it was a place he wanted to help look after. He felt his breath catch in his throat.

"Almost every culture has considered your world alive," Arren whispered.

"I think I might believe them," Chase mused.

***

An hour and a half later they landed and were in the entry ready to leave. After days of running around space Chase was looking forward to breathing his local air again.

"At least we now know the Universal Unity doesn't care much," he mumbled, "As long as we stay out of their territory, we're fine. If we can keep you a secret from the rest of Earth we should be fine here."

"Yeah, but we still have to worry out the Coebri," Lucky said.

"Oh yes!" Arren said, "And that's because – hang on, why is someone spraying anaesthetic on the door?[43]"

Suddenly, she yelped and a bright light cut a perfect circle around the normal door. It fell away to reveal the silhouette of a tall, bulky human with mechanised limbs, a glowing crystal eye and an odd limp. His boots were caked in mud and his clothes were covered with smudges of slick, black oil. On his shoulder, a little green Will-o perched, glowing menacingly.

Behind him, smiling a truly evil smile, was Mark T.

"Tzaarkh," Arren whispered in fear.

"Because..." the mechanised man finished for her, smiling a wicked smile. "The Coebri will stop at nothin', and go through anyone to get wha'ever is rightfully theirs."

---

[42] Anaesthetic is used to numb pain, say, before pulling out a splinter or sore tooth.

Chapter 12
The day the Coebri Pirates came to Ms Garibaldi's garden

There was a brief struggle, so brief Chase couldn't even tell what had happened. Arren and the Coebri pirate, Lord Tzaarkh, just twitched and stood there for a moment, then he laughed.

"You'd best be getting out of there, younglings. Can't 'ave ye dinting up me property anymore!"

"How'd you find me?" Arren said, probably stalling for time.

"I 'ad a little 'elp here," Tzaarkh teased, pushing a grinning and victorious Mark T forward and patting him on the back. "Seems we got ourselves a little Earth-man who knows 'ow to drive a deal! I was stuck, searching all over this blasted land, when this clever boy leads me right to ye. Something about an off page blog."

"He pays well." Mark T smiled. "Gave me $100 just to tell him where I saw you! Worth every cent," he said, looking like he was happier to hurt them than to earn anything for himself.

Arren looked defeated. "Come on," she said to Lucky and Chase.

They were just about to walk out when Tzaarkh suddenly stopped her.

"Not ye, dear."

"Hey, she's..." Chase began. He was about to say 'mine', but she stopped him with a look. Then Chase realised, he had no idea what the Coebri were capable of in order to reclaim what they thought was their property.

"You can't have her," Chase stuttered, "she's in our land now and we don't have slaves!"

"Aah, well, she won't be 'ere for long, will she?" Tzaarkh smiled a strange, filthy smile, his breath smelt like a dead possum.

"I wouldn't bet on that!" Another voice suddenly said over a megaphone. It sounded like officer Costa.

From all around Ms Garibaldi's junkyard, dozens of black clad elite Special Service troops swarmed, armed and alert. They had large rifles and they pointed them at Tzaarkh. Then from underneath a pile of trash, a fully loaded tank unexpectedly rolled out.

Someone has been busy, Chase had a random thought.

Costa continued, "Oh, and boys, just in case you're thinking about leaving without handing over the keys..." He said, and a floodlight lit up several meters away. In it, a dark, masked man held a gun to the brow of a scraggly headed person.

"Dad!" Lucky screamed.

"Boys!" He shouted in reply, "Don't do what they ask! There are too many lives at stake to risk them on me!"

What a hero, thought Chase reluctantly, desperately hoping he didn't have to find out what it was like to choose between your father and the world.

The Coebri captain laughed. "Still can't get yer act together, can ye, Earthlings. Soon enough you'll sign this 'ole world over to me people, then we'll 'ave some order around 'ere."

"As representatives of the Australian Government, we claim this ship as our own!" Costa demanded.

The Coebri captain laughed. "Oh, so it's a fight you're looking for, is it Earthling? That's an old Coebri property law. Winner takes the ship, but ... you sure you want to take on me and me entire crew?" He threatened.

Suddenly, from out of a nearby dimension, another six Coebri ships rolled in. They were small, probably only a man or two. But they were covered in laser guns, cannons and various other devices of mayhem and destruction.

This is getting serious, Chase thought, feeling the panic rise within him.

"You think this is our first date, Coebri scum!" Costa shouted. Suddenly a large energy field enveloped the tank, and all the Special Service soldiers fitted glowing green and ethereal attachments to their weapons.

The Coebri captain grew silent. "Now boys, we don't need things to get messy," he said, sounding just a little nervous.

"Not so tough, are you n–"

Suddenly there was an old lady's voice from amidst the garbage, "Ma chi fa questo macello?" It began.

It was Ms Garibaldi. She stumbled from her house, a dozen meters away. Then she saw the spaceships hovering over her yard.

"Oh santo cielo–" she began, but was cut short as a Coebri ship suddenly swung around to threaten her with a dozen menacing lasers.

"Call off yer dogs," Tzaarkh ordered Costa, threatening Ms Garibaldi's life if they didn't back down.

"Think we care?" Costa replied coldly.

Then Tzaarkh shoved Mark T towards Ms Garibaldi. She stopped him from falling face first into the dirt and helped him up.

"Hey!" He shouted, "We had a deal."

"And you've been paid." Tzaarkh shouted over him with an evil smile. He'd just added Mark T to the threat.

For a moment there was silence, the Coebri ship's glowing cannons making the air waiver with intense heat as it pointed its guns right at Mark T and Ms Garibaldi. Mark was visibly trembling, but Ms Garibaldi held her head up with dignity.

He hid his face against her shoulder.

"Non ti spaventi, fanciullo," she consoled him in a whisper, looking up at the ship with unstoppable courage. For the second time in his life, Chase found himself feeling sorry for Mark T.

There was silence. Costa just smiled darkly and pointed his gun right at Tzaarkh. No one was backing down. Tzaarkh stopped smiling, it seemed things we're not going the way he'd expected.

Now this is beyond serious, Chase thought, looking desperately for a way to escape.

Suddenly a Special Service soldier pointed upwards. "Look!"

He pointed up at a star and it took Chase a second to realise that the star was moving. It looked like a bright silver meteorite was hurtling towards Earth. It took only another second for it to reach the ground, crashing down in the centre of the two groups with a tumultuous thud. It was a man, a tall silver man of perfect proportions over two and a half meters tall. He landed on the ground like some kind of superhero and stood up, his glowing silver eyes scanning the two small armies.

But he only had one arm.

Costa swore. "Troops, stand down!"

The Special Service soldiers relocked their weapons and stood at attention.

But Tzaarkh looked grim.

" 'ello tracker," he said, "What brings you all the way out to this dung heap of a planet?"

The tracker looked around, then spoke in its cold, emotionless, mechanical voice.

"Coebri Admiral Tzaarkh, during my first unsuccessful attempt at returning unit 'Arrendrallendriania' to you, your claim of ownership was brought into question. In order to find evidence to support your claim for future confrontations, I researched your ownership rights among the Coebri. However, this act has served only to *further* bring into question the validity of your claims of ownership. Evidence indicates you are not the rightful owner of neither this vessel, nor of your mining rights among your own people."

"How dare ye!" Tzaarkh hissed, "I won them both fair and true in a game of chance an 'undred years ago!"

"Game of chance?" Arren questioned. It seemed to be news to her.

Before she could say anything else the tracker continued. "Furthermore, several of your activities in the region have cast doubt on the legitimacy of many of your ventures, even within the region of space controlled by the Universal Unity. I am required to search your ship's records. Also, before the right of your claim to ownership of this vessel–"

"You'll never take me alive!" He shouted. "Get 'im boys."

Immediately the Coebri ships swarmed the silver man, blasting at him with high energy rays of blue and green. They didn't miss, or perhaps the silver man didn't let them miss, protecting everything else with his own body. Swinging a single fist of silver he brought two of the Coebri ships down.

"Go the fire!" Tzaarkh shouted, and all the Coebri ships opened up with beams of burning yellow light. The silver man fell to one knee.

"That's pure energy from their ship cores!" Arren gasped. "They're desperate."

A Special Service soldier raised his weapon to help, but Costa held it down.

A second later, the silver man melted.

"So much for that help," Lucky groaned.

"Now!" Costa yelled and the Special Service guns went back up. "I happen to know that a core burn uses a lot of fuel and now your shields are down for the next half hour. Unless you want your heads filled with Earth titanium, enhanced with your own alien technology, you'll–"

The Coebri were at a disadvantage and everyone knew the Earthlings were ready to commit murder to get what they wanted.

"Stop!" Arren shouted. Her ship, or herself, shuddered completely into normal space. It was the largest object there, a giant jagged pyramid spaceship bigger than most school ovals, resting just above the junkyard. Everyone stared at it in amazement. Now when she spoke her voice seemed to come from everywhere.

"First. You Coebri. I'll take your law. If one of these Earthlings takes you on, one on one, will you surrender your rights to them if you lose?"

Tzaarkh smiled. "I'm liking this arrangement bettah."

It seemed a gunfight with alien-enhanced Earth soldiers wasn't to his taste after all.

"Yeah boss, show them Earthlings what we Coebri got!" one of them shouted.

The Special Service soldiers were nodding too. It was a pride battle, Earth versus Coebri.

Costa stood forward. He put on some black gloves and sheathed a Special Service knife into his boot. Tzaarkh cracked his knuckles then took a ball from his coat and tossed it into the air. It opened out to form a red curtain of light, a duelling arena with him in the centre beside the pool of molten tracker.

"Oh no, not Costa," Arren said suddenly.

"Hey!" the Federal Policeman protested.

"Lucky, go," Arren urged him in her normal voice.

"What?" He asked her.

"You're a warrior. You're already a warrior, just like all those guard wannabes. You understand conflict, and deception. Especially deception. *And* you know when to hold back, Costa won't. It's got to be you."

Lucky turned and looked at the bulky Coebri pirate. Then at the seething Federal Policemen threatening him with murder if he participated, or worse, lost.

But there was something in Lucky that just didn't know when to hold back.

He nodded. "How?"

Unexpectedly Arren blasted him from behind with a ball of glowing golden light. Lucky went flying from the spaceship and into the circle.

"Arrr!" Said Tzaarkh, "Ye were supposed to be saving that for me, child!"

Then she actually poked her tongue out at him in a timeless Earthling gesture of derision.

Costa was livid. He and his men moved around the field but couldn't get in. The Coebri moved about cautiously as well, picking up their fallen comrades, trying to keep the Earthlings out of arms reach.

"What did you..." Lucky said, looking at his hands.

"Remember, you are a warrior!" Arren yelled to him.

Then as soon as the others were all distracted, she erected a transparent force field around her ship.

"Go Earthlings!" She shouted.

"Don't let 'er get away!" Tzaarkh replied, and his ships moved to surround her.

Lucky was still just sitting there.

"Get up and fight him, boy!" Costa yelled, ripping off his Special Service gloves. "It's for your *planet*."

Lucky looked over at him and gave him a look which stated *I do not do this for you.*

"Let's just finish this quick like," the Coebri captain muttered and cautiously walked up to Lucky. His hand turned into a mace and he swung it down to crush him.

And missed. At the last minute, Lucky looked up and dove between the Coebri captain's legs. He leapt up like an athlete, looking back at his hands.

"What did you do?" He asked her once more.

"Changed you…" Arren whispered, her voice sounding sad.

Tzaarkh moved quickly, but Lucky jumped right over his head. He hit the force field and fell to the ground, but as he fell he turned and landed on his feet with almost no effort.

"Ouch!" he said.

"You'll feel a lot more than that when ye wear the slave collar!" Tzaarkh roared.

He turned around and tried to hit Lucky, but Lucky dodged and blocked his blows with his bare hands. It was like he was twenty times stronger, but he still took cuts and had no idea what he was doing.

"You know how to do this!" Arren shouted.

He looked at her.

He nodded.

The Coebri captain rushed to the attack, using every mechanical advantage he had. But Lucky was quicker and perfectly fit. He jumped up without effort and kneed Tzaarkh in the face.

The captain stumbled backwards and the Coebri looked nervous.

The Special Service troops cheered.

"Stay alert!" Costa yelled, then muttered under his breath, "I want that technology... I want it badly and I don't care *how I get it.*"

Then the battle inside the force field really got intense. Swinging and blocking like a martial arts expert, it was Lucky versus a transforming human machine. Tzaarkh ran in for another flurry just as Lucky went to kick him and Tzaarkh somehow accidently grabbed his foot. He went to smash Lucky into the ground, but Lucky twisted around and did a perfect push up against it instead. Then Lucky turned around again and smacked his other foot against Tzaarkh, breaking his mechanical hand right off. The Coebri pirate fell back in surprise.

For a moment, Arren looked away.

"Traitor! Thief! Ye kept all this back from me!" Tzaarkh roared at her.

"I *hate* you!" Arren screamed with sudden passion. "To you I am just a *slave*! You rob others using the law, and *you do not keep your word!*" She stated it like it was the most severe crime in the universe, and it probably was.

Then, just as Lucky was leaping into the air to make a flying kick at Tzaarkh, the devious captain snuck his foot against a special point in the field and it disappeared.

"The *cheat*," Arren whispered.

Everyone else was only just beginning to absorb that fact when Tzaarkh reached down, grabbed a car with his mechanically enhanced body, and threw it at Lucky.

It hit him head on. He managed to slip out from under it as it flew through the air, then it crashed into a pile of Ms Garibaldi's junk. Lucky toppled over and didn't get up.

Costa sucked in his breath to say something.

"Right!" Arren yelled, and the sky filled with lightning. Her voice became deeper and filled the air, like thunder. "I will *not* watch any longer. I will *not* be a slave. I will *not* be a tool. I will *not* be torn apart and used for research, my secrets becoming weapons humans use to kill each other!"

A bright white light exploded from Arren and everyone was thrown to the ground.

"Take her out!" Costa yelled from the ground. A dozen alien-enhanced Earthling bullets sped towards her but they were too late. They all burnt up in the light she was emitting, her eyes burning like fire. Chase had no idea how he was able to survive the brilliant light. Then, when she spoke, it shook the ground, and once again her voice came from everywhere.

"Earthlings. You are not ready. You celebrate violence. You oppress your own race. You poison your world. I judge you unready. You are not ready. *You are not ready!!*"

Brilliant bolts of white lightning shot from the spaceship and scarred the earth. They made Costa's black car explode. They tore the weapons from the soldiers grip. They cut the tank clean in half.

"Pull back, pull back!" Costa yelled.

She continued, "Coebri. You are dishonest. You oppress the innocent. You have turned from higher laws. I judge you unworthy. *You are not worthy!!*"

They tried to stop her, to shoot her with the blue and green lasers, but they couldn't penetrate the halo of light around her. The lightning only cut two or three of their ships apart but it was enough. They began to retreat, one of them swooping down to scoop up Tzaarkh.

"You will be mine, child!" He promised and she blasted one of his engines to pieces.

Chase sighed in great relief. It was over. Or...

It should be over, but the halo of light still continued to grow. In its incredible brightness Chase could see citizens coming out of their houses. Everyone was looking up at the glowing spaceship floating in the night sky.

Then Chase saw the first few fires. As the white halo began to touch the highest of Ms Garibaldi's rubbish it was crumpling like paper and catching fire. The light continued to grow, soon it would touch the ground, it would touch the school, it would touch Lucky.

"Arren, stop! You did it, you need to stop now!"

But the light did not stop.

Her voice of judgement and thunder continued, "Everywhere I look, they're fighting. This world is full of pollution and violence and lies. But I can fix it up. I can fix it all..."

The ground below began to crumple under the white flame.

Chase looked up at her. She was burning like some kind of nuclear reactor and if he didn't do something, she would destroy the world.

His world.

He didn't know what to do. All his life, someone else had been around to tell him what was going to happen, or what to do, or what he was supposed to feel. But now it was only him and he could do nothing, unless he helped her stop herself. So he just opened his mouth and started talking.

"Arren, no," he stumbled to find the words, "I know. All you say is true, but... we... we're *trying* Arren. Trying to be better! Can you see that? I know it doesn't amount to much yet... but, please. Please! Have patience. We're *trying*," he said, pushing back his own tears.

She looked over to him, still glowing with fire.

And smiled.

"Yes, yes. You are all still trying ... and there is still time..."

The light stopped growing.

Huge chunks of broken spaceships, tanks and guns began to float upwards, anything with advanced technology, and Arren took it into the hull. The bright light coalesced around her.

"Cover your ears," she said.

He pressed the palms of his hands over his ears, scrunching his tear rimmed eyes shut. Suddenly, there was a thunderous crash, like lightning striking the ground right next to him. Inside his mind he thought he heard a voice, Arren's voice.

Wow, what a storm! I think lightning hit poor Ms Garibaldi's place... She suggested.

Then it was dark, and it started to rain.

When he opened his eyes the ship was invisible again. He could see people walking around in a daze, many of them lying down as if they'd just decided to take a nap in the rain. The Coebri and Federal Police were nowhere to be seen. Lucky was all right, struggling to sit up with Dad's help. But Arren, Arren the girl, was lying quietly on her side in the door of her spaceship. She was not moving and did not make a sound.

"Arren! Are you all right?"

She did not reply.

"Arren!" He cried, tapping her on her cheek. It was soft and warm. So soft. She lay perfectly quiet on the floor and she felt limp. He tried to feel for her breath but there was none.

"Arren! No!" He shouted to the rain.

She didn't move. He reached out and tried to feel for a pulse on her wrist but he could find none. She was... she was...

He grabbed her hand and started crying again, his tears falling onto her hand. He didn't see Lucky standing up and watching. But he didn't care who saw. For once in his life he didn't care if others saw how he felt, he just didn't want to lose his friend.

"Oh," a girl's voice said suddenly.

Chase pulled himself together, blinking away his tears. Arren stirred.

"Chase," she said in wonder, "You're holding my hand."

He gripped it tightly and laughed, and didn't let go.

As she stumbled to her feet, he helped her stand up. She looked out at the damaged land.

"What … have I become?" She muttered, her voice filled with sorrow.

"Arren, you did it!" He tried to cheer her up, while wiping his tears. "You fought off the soldiers, you beat back the Coebri. You… you are your own master now. You won your freedom."

She blinked in surprise.

"You, relinquish your claim on me too?" She asked.

"Yes, always did. No one can own *you*."

She smiled broadly. "Then… then I am free… it is *good* to be on Earth," she said.

They were still holding hands. From down on the ground Lucky gave them a thumbs up.

"You're not letting go?" she asked Chase with a smile.

He grinned. "Let him think what he wants. I am your friend," he said and squeezed her hand.

They stood in the rain. After a pause he sighed with relief and said what he'd always said, "So, what happens now?"

She laughed. "I guess … we go back to school."

"School! You're an advanced alien spaceship…"

"And you're a planet in need of a good example. Come on Chase, let's go home and then next week, we're going to go to school. Oh! And how about on the weekend we go win that *rocket contest!*"

Sure, save the world, win a rocket contest... Chase had to laugh. She sure had some interesting priorities, his best friend from outer space!

End of Book 1 *and* Start of Book 2
Freedom and Rockets

There was no cheating, no alien technology, just good, simple rocket science!

Lucky and Arren sat on the fence at Ms Garibaldi's the next Sunday. Chase was standing around and they were waiting for Mark T to turn up.

"Now *that* was a weird week," Chase summed up.

"Understatement!" Lucky agreed.

"How's everyone doing?" Arren asked.

Chase could tell she was still feeling guilty about what she'd done to make everyone forget. It was much worse than simple hypnosis. Everyone who heard the thunder seemed unable to remember a thing, except for Chase and his family. Everyone else had a headache the whole next day, but most people didn't seem to think much of it. Nearly the whole neighbourhood checked in at poor Ms Garibaldi's place to see how she was doing. Even she was convinced that lightning had struck, setting fire to several things and even miraculously throwing a car several meters from where it used to be. Of course, now she had hundreds of new people to talk to, for hours on end, so she was happier than ever.

They hadn't heard a thing from the Federal Police, if that's what they really were, and from Arren's searching of the internet there wasn't much to be found there either.

As for the Coebri, not even a whisper. But Chase was sure they were out there, biding their time.

The world hadn't changed a bit. Everyone kept on doing what they'd always done. But the three of them had changed.

Lucky could all but fly now, and Chase had to keep telling him to keep his great strength and agility under control or people would get suspicious. Arren told them it wasn't anything he wasn't able to do already but just a tune up, just a bringing out of all his natural talent. But he was like a body builder, martial arts expert and pro dancer all in one. He could run upside down on the roof, or make it look like he could. He loved it.

Arren was confident now, making less mistakes. She seemed to love school a lot. Her favourite class was Civics and Citizenship and she even got an award for an incredibly passionate and persuasive letter to the editor of a local newspaper about recycling. She was a wiz with her hands; people were always coming to her to fix up their phones and computers, and she always did.

As for Chase, well, he felt changes in himself as well - more alert, more aware. Less bothered by what others thought of him, more confident about who he was and what he wanted. Superpowers, perhaps, but of the more quiet kind.

"Still, nothing you couldn't already do at your best, if you believed in yourself," Arren said as they waited.

"Yeah, but what our government wouldn't give to get their hands on that!" Chase said looking at Lucky enjoying one armed hand stands. "They'd build super warriors. Then they'd probably invade somewhere."

"Or more likely," Arren offered, "They'd oppress other countries' technologies and economies, and use their super soldiers to keep their own people blissfully unaware of the crimes done in the name of national peace."

"They'd do that?" he asked.

"But in a world that chooses violence," she asked, "is it occasionally necessary?"

Chase wasn't sure that two wrongs made a right. Philosophy was Arren's favourite topic and she could go on about it for hours, so perhaps it was good that Mark T and his lackeys finally turned up then.

Mark T gave them a greasy look, especially Arren, who returned a cheeky smile and wave. They weren't too sure how much he knew, or how much he remembered, but they all agreed he was a danger now. He'd brought the Coebri pirate Lord Tzaarkh right to them, putting them in real danger for his own benefit.

Putting the whole Earth in jeopardy.

"What ya got for me this week, Chase," Mark T growled, folding his arms.

"What, no insults?" Chase smiled.

Mark T said nothing.

Chase put down his rocket in his perfectly restored rocket launcher, Arren really was *amazing* at fixing things. "I've learnt a few things since we last met, Nemesis," he crowed.

"The name's Mark T!" The bully shouted.

Chase was silent, clearly ancient Greek or modern English weren't Mark's strong points. Nemesis wasn't an insult, it was the ancient Greek goddess of... oh, forget it.[44]

"Anyway, Mark T... you ever heard of Newton's third law?"

Mark T didn't pause, "To every action there is an equal and opposite reaction."

"Glad to see you're still paying attention!" Chase teased to lighten the mood. Mark T was one of the few people who could be relied on to know that.

---

[43] <u>Nemesis</u> – an arch enemy, derived from the goddess of retribution in Greek mythology.

Chase set down his rocket. This time, it was almost half-full of water. Dense, heavy tap water.

Mark laughed.

"All that water'll just hold your rocket down!" he mocked.

"I thought that too, but it actually gives the air more to push out. And a greater downwards force means a greater upwards force."

"Che bravo!" Arren clapped.

"Shut it, Sheila," Mark T said rudely.

She raised an eyebrow at him, annoyed, but seemed to decide a reply was beneath her. Lucky, however, nearly jumped off the pole and decked him.

But Chase just laughed. The insults were no more than water off a ducks back to him now; it was the science that mattered.

"Let's let our rockets do the talking," he grinned.

Mark T had 'improved' his rocket, adding some dangerous caustic soda to the mix. But it didn't lift off any higher than last week, the air pressure inside wasn't any greater, even if it did build up quicker. He still seemed pleased with himself.

But when Chase's turn came, pumping with a foot pump this time, his rocket half-full of water more than doubled Mark's best. It shot up into the air leaving behind a glorious stream of water, little droplets dancing down to form a faint rainbow. He'd won!

"How...?" Mark T and his lackeys wondered.

"What won was not the air pressure alone; we both have the same air pressure. What I needed was water in the bottle, something for the air to push down, giving the rocket stronger force up..."

"That's rot!" Mark T protested. "You must have cheated!"

"I wonder how you substantiate that claim?" Arren asked, knowing it would just make him angry.

Chase laughed. "Keep the five dollars, it's just not worth it."

Mark T shoved him and grabbed the pump out of his hand.

Chase didn't mind, didn't even get angry. He'd already won.

Arren had to hold Lucky back from disarming Mark T and probably knocking him off his feet.

"There is one other factor, *space nerd*," Mark T mocked. "That's how hard you push the cork in. Makes it build up more force."

"Yes, I think that would be true," Chase agreed, just not upset.

Mark T, however, was really angry. The kind of angry one gets when they're ready to do something stupid. Something really, really stupid. His face was red and his knuckles white. He took the cork off the pump, marched over to Ms Garibaldi's fence and wedged his bottle in a suitable crack. He filled it half-full with water. Then he grabbed a nearby piece of metal piping, there was plenty around the old junkyard, and bashed the cork in hard.

Really, really hard.

"Ahh, Mark T–" Arren said.

"Shut it!" he told her.

Chase could see the problem as well.

"Mark…"

He swung around and threatened them with the pipe. "Shut yer yap, or do you want me to shut it with this?" he shouted.

Chase just stood there, unfazed about what Mark T said, but just a little concerned about what Mark thought he was going to do.

Mark T marched over to the launcher and twisted the foot pump back into the cork; which must have been quite difficult to do considering how firmly it was wedged in now.

Chase stood well back.

"Ahh, Mark..." one of his lackey's said, sounding worried.

"Would everyone just SHUT UP!" he roared.

He was pumping furiously. Air was pouring obediently into the bottle. Then it slowed down as the pressure inside the bottle increased, and increased.

Everyone else backed away.

"Fools!" Mark T shouted, pushing harder and harder to get the air into the bottle. "You think I don't know what I'm doing? I'm a science *genius*, unlike *you* Chase! And I'll never–"

And that was when the bottle *exploded*.

Now, there'd been quite a few explosions in the past week, but none of them sounded like a pipe bomb going off in someone's back yard. The pressure, or the surprise, knocked Mark T right off his feet. Everyone's ears were ringing.[45]

Mark T was so stunned that for the first few minutes he couldn't even sit up. When he finally came to his senses, his lackeys coaxing him up, he burst uncontrollably into tears. Lucky couldn't stop laughing but Chase ran and got him a drink and Arren rubbed his back till he pulled himself together.

---

[45] Those little bouncing balls of air pressure can be pretty strong, eh! Enough of them can pop a balloon, explode a bottle or even lift up a car (what do you think tires are full of...?)

Eventually he stumbled off, leaning on his lackeys.

"We'll get them next time," he said dazedly.

"Think he'll be all right?" Chase wondered.

"Fortunately, minor damage," Arren said. "It's lucky he wasn't standing over the bottle or we'd be taking him to hospital now. That was downright dangerous."[46]

"What?" Lucky laughed. He held out the cork, the plastic bottle top still wrapped around it. He'd caught it in mid-explosion. "He *deserves* it."

Chase did not feel convinced, "I fear it'll make him hate us more," he sighed.

"Come on guys, it's getting late," Arren said, "Let's go home."

***

Home. Home had changed too. Arren had taken over their parent's old room and Dad was now keeping the whole house clean while sleeping on the couch, making dinner almost every night. He still made out like he didn't know what was going on but they knew he remembered. And every now and then they'd catch him staring at Arren, probably still trying to see her aura. By the time they got home he was waiting for them on the front porch.

"Hey kids, dinner again!" he called out in a cheery voice. His hair was tied back in a neat ponytail and he had on a new coat they'd not seen before.

"Where'd you get that, Dad?" Lucky asked.

He smiled. "Remember, well, remember that incident recently? Seems I tore my old coat quite a bit. I found this

---

[46] Yes, yes it was. Bottle rockets are dangerous enough to do *serious* damage, like broken bones or popped eyes. **Do not** attempt them without proper *safety* and *responsible* adult help.

old one in the closet while cleaning up this week and it still fits perfectly."

"What, one of those Federal Police guys tore up your favourite dressing gown?" Lucky said, unimpressed, probably planning some kind of revenge against them.

Dad looked serious. "Forget them son. You don't... don't even mention..."

Arren suddenly looked up. "Speaking of trouble!" she stated and ran to the doorway to stand behind them all.

A moment later a black car pulled up in front of the house. Two tall men in dark suits got out. It was Flannigan, he was smiling, and Costa, he was *not* smiling.

And then there was a third person. A woman. A neat, professional woman. Chase thought she looked strangely familiar, though she terrified him in ways he couldn't explain. Her hair was raven black, pulled back in a business-like bun. She wore a porcelain smile, but there was no human kindness in her eyes. Chase knew right away she was dangerous. The air seemed to get cold around her, and she got out of the passenger's seat like a heartless executioner arriving at work.

"Who's that?" Arren asked them.

"Elizabeth?" Dad said, voice cracking with disbelief.

"Who's Elizabeth?" Arren asked.

Only Chase could find his voice enough to speak, the sound rasping out of disbelieving lungs. "Mum?!"

The story continues in book 2, "Elizabeth" ...

Feedback and comments are always welcome Arren@drjoe.id.au

What Ms Garibaldi said

'Garibaldi' is an Italian surname, and the surname of a famous Italian army general who managed to unite the states of Italy into one solid country. He is often considered the father of Italy. Here are the Ms Garibaldi quotes, my translation, and the literal translation because it's so much fun and helps us to realise how tricky it is to translate between languages:

"Ma che c'e'?" = "Who's there?" (Literally 'But what there is!')

"Ui, ragazzo! Vai via, subito!" = "Hey, kid! Get lost, now!" (Literally 'hey, boy! Go away, now!')

"Scemo." = "Idiot" (Literally, 'Stupid.')

"Questi figli mi fanno sempre stancare." = "These kids always make me tired." (Literally 'These children always make me tired.')

"Che cosa?" = "What?" (Literally 'That there is?')

"Ma chi fa questo macello?" = "Who's making all that noise?" (Literally 'But who does all this mess.')

"Oh santo cielo-" = "Oh my gosh!" (Literally 'Oh holy heavens.')

"Non ti spaventi, fanciullo," = "Have no fear, child." (Literally 'Don't fear yourself, little one.')

About the author

Dr Joe (AKA Dr Joseph Ireland) is a touring science presenter with a Doctorate in the Philosophy of Science Education. He is a fan of fantasy, devout Christian, and loves spending time with his wonderful wife and delightful daughters. He finds life's purpose in challenging people in the way they think and what they think about what they think they think. He also plays flute.

If you're looking for a science show for your school why not visit www.drjoe.id.au to find out more!

Space Chase - Arrendrallendriania

More wonderful titles by Dr Joe & Creating Science:

Delightful high fantasy for the thoughtful young reader
Choice, set free 1: Quest of the Tae'anaryn
Choice, set free 2: The Wizard's Apprentice
Choice, set free 3: The Paladin's Squire
Choice, set free 4: The Enchantress's Chrysalis
Choice, set free 5: The Spear of the Troll Prince

An engaging science fiction adventure that introduces real science concepts to readers.
Space Chase 1: Arrendrallendriania
Space Chase 2: Elizabeth
Space Chase 3: Daniel
Space Chase 4: The Mechanizer

Thrilling young adult science fantasy adventure.
The Dragon Riders of Pearl
The Dragon Riders of Pearl 2: Seven Worlds
The Dragon Riders of Pearl 3: Return of the Plague
The Dragon Riders of Pearl 4: Rage of the Dragonmen
The Dragon Riders of Pearl 5: Twilight of the Giants

And for the budding scientist:
<u>Creating Science –</u>
<u>Dr Joe's book of scientific experiments and activities</u>

Place your mark here each time you read this book!

www.ingramcontent.com/pod-product-compliance
Lightning Source LLC
Chambersburg PA
CBHW051436290426
44109CB00016B/1580